Beyond Brand

Why it's the **experience**
that causes people to fall in
love with your **brand!**

CRAIG MCVOY

R3THINK PRESS

First published in Great Britain 2018
by Rethink Press (www.rethinkpress.com)

This book is dedicated to
Robert Faulconbridge

Like a second father to me, you were always an amazing support.

You sadly didn't get to see it in print, but I hope you are proud of the finished article.

Rest in Peace, Bob. We all miss you so very much.

Praise

In the modern world of global competitive business, developing, protecting and projecting your brand and enhancing the customer experience is critical. The unprecedented disruption the global economy has experienced over the last decade, and will almost certainly continue to see, means this is very important. During my career at John Lewis, this dedication to brand, reputation and the customer experience was fundamental to our success. This book is an enlightening and engaging exploration of many themes I recognise from experience and I wholeheartedly recommend it, no matter what sector or business you are in.

Andy Street
Mayor of the West Midlands and
Former CEO of John Lewis

The seven principles in this book are foundational to the success of your brand, and the new competitive advantage. Craig teaches a framework that can be used by a business of any size to improve the experience its customers and employees receive. If you want to attract more customers and then keep them for longer, this book gives you the steps required to deliver this.

Shep Hyken
Customer service expert and *New York Times*
bestselling author of *The Amazement Revolution*

The new battleground for customer loyalty isn't product, it's the experience your customers have with your products and with you as an organisation. Craig's book provides a powerful framework, backed by data, real-life case studies and practical tools, to identify and rectify failure points in the customer experience. It's a must-read for marketers, customer experience practitioners and executives alike.

Matthew Dixon
Co-author of *The Effortless Experience*
and *The Challenger Sale*

Every business's ideal customer isn't an *engaged* one. It's a *loyal* one. Someone who buys. Who keeps buying. And who tells their contacts to buy too. And you'll only get these customers if you give them an incredible experience so that they crave more. Craig's excellent book gives you step-by-step guidance on how to do just that. A revelation.

Andy Bounds
Sales expert, award-winning consultant and
best-selling author of *The Jelly Effect*

Craig has written what should have been my next book! I spent the last third of my career fighting the misconception that brand was just the logo, was just the advertising or the marketing, but it is in fact the reflection of an organisation's culture, of their people.

In *Beyond Brand*, McVoy takes the argument well beyond that the 'experience' is key; it's what presents the culture and creates customers for life. Beyond that, he packages it in a practical 'how to book' any size organisation and all business leaders can use and leverage. Thanks Craig! I can retire.

Ted Matthews
Best selling author of *Brand: It ain't the logo.*
It's what people think of you

This book is an exciting mini-MBA but centred around the right thing: customers, as opposed to finance. It is packed with stories that are memorable, and in there, a stern warning for any company that doesn't pay enough attention to the customer experience: consumers wouldn't mind if 74% of brands fell off the face of the earth!

Nigel Shanahan
Founder, Rant & Rave

As the business world plummets headlong into dealing with an era of 'everyone knowing everything instantly', what people, customers and employees know (or experience) from brands will increasingly shape their desire to engage, or disengage with them. *Beyond Brand* is a useful read to understand this continuing shift to the 'Experience Economy' and to help ensure you and your business aren't left behind."

Will King
Founder, King of Shaves

The very best of business thinking and case studies put into a practical strategy that all businesses can use to stand out from the competition.

Derek Williams
Founder, The WOW Awards

An invaluable, thought provoking read with great tips on what to do to improve your Customer Strategy.

Philip Hesketh
Award-winning professional speaker on the psychology of persuasion and influence and best selling author of *How to Persuade and Influence People* and *Persuade*

Today's marketplace is so crowded that consumers have lots of choice and have therefore become very savvy with the brands they like to associate with, the level of service they expect and the price they are prepared to pay. As we find certain brands that we recognise and become comfortable with, we tend to stick with them once we know they match our vision and values. We pride ourselves on upholding the values we care about and that our customers care about too, always doing our best to match and exceed their expectations. This book provides valuable insight into the importance of building credibility with your target market and how to invest in an experience that means consumers fall in love with your brand.

Dr Jason Wouhra OBE
Chairman, Institute of Directors West Midlands;
Director, East End Foods plc

Timely, relevant and true, *Beyond Brand* makes a compelling case that it's not what you do, it's how you do it that matters.

Jay Baer
Founder, Convince & Convert and
author of *Hug Your Haters*

There is no doubt that building a scalable and profitable business that attracts increasing numbers of customers, keeps them buying and referring others to your door, requires a recognition that the market never stands still. Standing out from the crowd is more than being the first to launch the next shiny new thing; it requires a deep understanding of brand values. Too often, business owners fail to understand their value proposition in terms of what problems they are solving for their customers and the benefits it brings to the market. This book provides an invaluable and accessible walk through some of the important lessons that makes a brand 'sticky' in very tight markets, especially on the national and international stage.

Professor Mark Hart
Deputy Director, Enterprise Research Centre;
Professor of Small Business and Entrepreneurship,
Aston Business School

What I love about this book is how Craig breaks down the term 'engagement' in a way that can help anyone understand why getting the attention of your customer is no longer enough to win their business. If you're looking for a logical process to help you create the right experience for earning and retaining more customers for your business, this book is a great starting point.

J.T. O'Donnell
Founder & CEO, Work It Daily

I am continuously astounded to see how many companies allocate the marketing budgets in promoting their brands to attract more customers but fail to understand that if they don't invest in their people and the culture within their business the initial brand building investment is wasted. In this book Craig has managed to explain in a simple step-by-step guide an understanding of the customer journey and the necessity of getting this right. It is a go-to business manual and applies to all sizes of businesses, relevant for start-up, SME though to the major corporates.

Chris Honer
CEO, JCB Paint

In the speed of day to day business life it's easy to forget that you are not the first to tread this path in the good or not so good times! *Beyond Brand* takes you on a journey reminding you of the things which are important to your employees and your clients, with some famous examples of success and failure. Fabulous read with some excellent exercises to use with each of the principles discussed in any business type.

Mark Abbott
Managing Director, Ansell Lighting

Contents

Introduction:
The Seven Principles

Business is changing

The last five years have seen a significant shift in the important factors which guarantee that a business survives, let alone thrives. Sure, the marketplace shows positive signs of becoming buoyant again after the recession, with economies growing, stock markets climbing and employment stable, but the security of individual companies has never been more uncertain. Those companies who are unprepared or unable to adapt to new market realities are being put under severe pressure to meet the growing expectations from both customers and employees.

Several factors define the fate of companies. These include:

- ⚙ The modern customer's expectation for things to be faster, more personal and more bespoke to meet their needs
- ⚙ The impact of the digital age, tightening the competition on the high street and reducing footfall in physical stores
- ⚙ Niche players, start-ups and new entrants snatching market share, affecting customer retention, and reducing margins and share of wallet.

On top of this, large corporates are throwing money at retaining their dominance in their traditional sectors, as well as expanding and diversifying into new areas.

The challenge to do well is certainly a tough one.

Some companies will have to take bold action if they are to progress and retain relevance; others will see the quiet but real deterioration of their businesses. The latter will face huge risks if they just hold on to what made them successful in the past as new expectations take a grip on what is now expected from a brand.

Doing what you've always done is not an option any more. Before, you could differentiate with a decent product or service, simply because it was difficult for customers to find other alternatives. Not so today. It's now much easier for customers to find good businesses with quality products, slick processes, and great people. The scale of competition in the market is affecting selling price, impacting profit, and causing margin erosion. Longstanding and proven business models are being replaced by new, agile companies who don't have the legacy baggage to deal with.

Today, with the advancements in technology, it is cheaper and easier for people to start a business in your sector. Amazon has moved the bar for all of us in terms of speed of delivery, inventory management, and meeting customer expectations. You need to make it simple and enjoyable for the customer to do business with your company, or they will choose to go elsewhere. And with political and economic challenges continuing to disrupt businesses, there are many hurdles to overcome that are not even in your control. With China reducing the cost of manufacturing and advancements in delivery methods, products can be copied in weeks. Big corporates have huge marketing and advertising budgets, so it is almost impossible for other companies to compete sustainably on the basis of pay per click (PPC) and search engine optimisation (SEO). Having a digital footprint and a good website are just par for the course; they won't differentiate you from your competition or bring loyalty to your business for long-term success. It's time to stop trying all the things that previously gave you a chance of beating the big budgets, they won't work anymore.

So what can you do in your business right now to thrive and grow in today's marketplace? If you are prepared to take action, where do you start?

There is one approach that is proven to deliver long-term, sustainable growth and brand value, whatever the size of your business – so much so, that expert analysts at Gartner, Walker and Forrester have predicted it will become the number one way to differentiate your brand by 2020. In today's world, product and price are pretty much the same across most competitors, so people now choose to buy from a company because of how it *feels* to do business with them. It is the emotional connection that you build through the experience you offer that affects customer loyalty, repeat purchase and retention more than any other factor.

Brand experience

Loyalty is what all companies want. The experience that makes customers 'sticky' to your brand, where value is found, is pivotal to long-term sustainable success. You won't get that from a product or service, you'll get that because of the way you make someone feel. It needs to be personal, it needs to be different, and it needs to be consistent. Truly great companies inspire people to choose them over the crowded market.

The global market spent $4.36 billion on customer experience initiatives in 2015, and this figure is projected to grow to $10.77 billion by 2020.[1] Customer experience is big business, and most companies are now investing in it, but you cannot 'half commit'. It is a proposition that requires an 'all in' approach, and for many companies it is their only hope of breaking away from the traditional marketing tactics threatening to drag them down. You may invest significantly in your branding and your marketing, but if the experience doesn't live up to it, then you will have wasted your money.

You need to lead the pack. You could wait for one of your competitors to do this first, or a start-up could enter your market with a fresh approach. But if you do wait for someone else to differentiate before you do, how many of your current customers will remain loyal to you? Whether your aim is to grow your business to sell it to a major industry player, or to continue to have a successful business for yourself, there is no denying that improving the customer experience will enable you to thrive as well as survive. This approach works for every business, from those feeling the pressure of market impact to those just starting to grow. You could be the one in your industry to set the new benchmark for customer experience. This could be where you take competitive advantage. This is something that businesses of all sizes need to consider if they are to continue to be relevant in their market in future years.

---

1   https://www.marketsandmarkets.com/PressReleases/customer-experience-management.asp

Until I created the Beyond Brand methodology, there wasn't a model for businesses of *all* sizes to use, a model that will improve their brand experience so they can deliver a better commercial performance as well as design a better experience for their customers.

There are consultancies who use their own approaches to work with the larger corporates, but they generally want a six-figure outlay before they will help. I wanted a methodology that was accessible to businesses of all sizes and will be as relevant in twenty years' time as it is today.

The Beyond Brand framework consists of seven principles:

1. **Purpose** – What is the reason that you exist as a business? What is it that you stand for?

2. **Audiences** – Who are the people you want your brand to connect with?

3. **Approach** – What methods do you use to reach your audiences, so that you make the right connections?

4. **Channels** – Which channels do you use to communicate with your audiences?

5. **Offer** – What do you provide that is unique to the rest of the market?

6. **Advantage** – How do you use insights and data to give you a competitive edge in building an emotional connection with your audience?

7. **Evolution** – Do you invest in continuous development to ensure that your business proposition improves people's lives?

These seven principles help you to review the effectiveness of your brand experience with your customers and employees. They are used throughout the three phases of your brand experience development:

1. **Discovery** – Reviewing where your current brand experience is today

2. **Design** – Developing your new brand experience

3. **Delivery** – Implementing the new design into your business with an effective plan

Where do you start? This book will take you through each of the seven principles that you need to consider as you work through those three phases. It will explain important considerations for each principle, showing how they make a difference to the experience you provide. I have included

exercises for you to complete at various checkpoints, to help you to identify the areas in your business that you need to get started on straight away. There are downloadable templates for you to use for these exercises, which you can access at www.beyondbrand.org/BBMTemplates.

By the end of the book, you will have everything you need to recognise the possibilities that are open to you and the advantages you could have today in your business, helping you to remain one step ahead of your competition.

With that in mind, let's take a look at the first principle of the Beyond Brand methodology.

Principle One

PURPOSE

X into Y

'There is only one valid definition of a business purpose: to create a customer.'

Peter Drucker

Purpose: The reason for which something is done or created or for which something exists.

Why do you exist? Not an easy question to answer. We are not talking about what you sell, or what services you offer, but what your company's overarching reason for existing is. What difference are you making that your competition just cannot replace? Why would the world be any different if you didn't exist?

We now live in a world where the choices customers have are greater than any time in history. Customers are spoilt for choice as to where to place their hard-earned cash. With the advance of technology, smaller, more agile businesses can now compete on a level playing field with the corporate giants who previously dominated these hugely competitive markets. It is now easier than it ever has been for businesses to challenge the market leaders, offering a product that competes, or undercutting the price.

In this digital world, people want convenience, and their expectations of service are higher than ever. Product placement can be anywhere and everywhere so easily, with advertising streams and traditional shopping methods being superseded by new channels that enable you to buy when you want and how you want. In order to thrive in today's markets, you need to connect with people on a much deeper level. Truly great companies do this by connecting with people about why they exist and why they should associate with them. People want to connect with a company that stands for the same values they do, and delivers these values consistently whenever they interact with the brand.

Building a brand is much more than just building a product suite and a logo. It is about building a brand promise that explains why your company exists and how you bring that 'why' alive in everything you do. It is a foundation that must be seen, felt and heard by your employees. Your 'why' is the personality of your brand coming to life in the experience, and its purpose needs to resonate with customers and potential customers.

It is the reason why people are prepared to wait twenty-four hours outside an Apple store for a new product when it is launched, why people remain loyal when a new product from a challenger brand comes to market, and why they are prepared to put up with the niggles they have to work around to use a product. They need to feel emotionally connected to your brand. People need to get it.

In the same way that you cannot easily explain why you love the person you choose to spend your life with, you can't always explain why you connect with a brand that you let into your life. You can guarantee, though, it will feel right in your gut, and those 'love brands' are what we all need to aspire to create.

If you want a customer to remain with your company, you need to think about the 'why', not just what you deliver for them. They need to feel emotionally connected to your brand. Simon Sinek built his reputation on his fantastic book *Start With Why*, and I would highly recommend that you watch his TED talk on the topic https://youtu.be/u4ZoJKF_VuA.

So, is your brand worth talking about? Does it stand for something that resonates with people? Does it have a social cause that people connect with? Does your brand culture come alive in the employee experience? Does it translate to the external market so your customers feel it too? It needs to be personal, different and consistent in the way that it is delivered.

According to a survey by Deloitte, organisations that focus beyond profit and instil a strong sense of purpose among their employees are more likely to find long-term success.[2] Whatever your USP (unique selling point), the consistency with which you execute your brand promise needs to flow through every channel you use and in every message you send out. This is why marketers are obsessed with something being 'on brand' and why agencies exist to deliver your purpose through your communications strategy. If something doesn't fit with your brand promise, it confuses your employees and customers, as it conflicts with your messaging. It would be the equivalent of Pret A Manger throwing away sandwiches, or Volvo producing a car with a one-star crash rating. It would conflict with their brand promise. Consistency in every interaction will either add or detract from the strength of your brand advocacy.

---

2   https://www2.deloitte.com/us/en/pages/about-deloitte/articles/culture-of-purpose.html

Your brand promise has to be genuine and sincere, and not just about 'making a load of money'. It has to shape your whole proposition, your culture and your future direction. Get it right and people will align with you. Get it wrong, though, and people will see straight through it, which could be fatal to your brand's reputation.

Good examples that enable us to align immediately with the brand through their communication are Zappos ('Deliver happiness to the world') and IKEA ('Make everyday life better'). Bad examples don't create any kind of emotional connection or loyalty to a brand and can support our bias against corporate enterprises, such as HP ('Kill the competition'), or GE ('Become number one in each category').

Creating and protecting your brand experience, then, is one of your most crucial tasks, and getting the buy-in of staff and customers is a huge part of that. Stories sell the brand experience and whether they come from people aspiring to work for you, or customers remaining loyal to you, the consistent quality of those stories will be one of the most valuable things you can invest in. A brand will live or die with the actions of every employee, so the employee experience and culture of the workplace are key for the leadership team to deliver. Your brand strategy doesn't need to focus on products or services as its key differentiator, the experiences alone will deliver the customer and employee advocacy that will create greatness. The brand experience is therefore so much more than marketing or advertising.

Perception

> *'Brand is just a perception, and perception will match reality over time. Sometimes it will be ahead, other times it will be behind, but brand is simply a collective impression some have about a product.'*
>
> **Elon Musk**

So, perception is reality then, even if it isn't the truth? How you are viewed by your customers is the difference between success and failure for your business. It doesn't matter if this perception isn't reality, because in the customers' minds it is. As businesses grow, this becomes increasingly difficult to manage, which is why even the smallest difference from what actually happened can now be the new reality, spreading far and wide across audiences and communities. Gerald Ratner, formerly chief executive of major British jewellery company Ratner's Group, famously once joked during a speech about the quality of two of the products the group sold. He didn't say that all his products were crap; he just made two jokes about the quality of two of the products he sold – two products out of a catalogue of thousands, yet within ten seconds, the public perception was that all of his products were crap. The joke wiped £500 million off the share value of the company: this PR disaster sent the world's largest jeweller close to collapse.

Perception can be viewed in the context of three distinct audiences, each of which needs to be managed within your brand experience:

* Your customers
* Your employees
* Your community

Customers. Do you know who your customers are? How well do you know them? Do you know what they value, their opinions and their buying habits?

Knowing your customers is about understanding the different customer avatars you have in your business thoroughly. This enables you to shape your products and services around their wants and needs. One of the major elements of growing your business is understanding who you want as customers, and equally who you don't want. You cannot appeal to everyone – if you do, you specialise in no one. If you are a dentist and you engage a PR agency, you want to work with one that specialises in helping dentists, one who understands your target market and knows everyone in your industry, including the journalists and media contacts who want to get a story. The same is true for your customers.

This doesn't mean that you only have one type of customer avatar; there may be several who make up your customer base. However, there should be something that links all your customers to your brand and makes them choose you instead of the other options in the market. Customers build a perception of your brand over time, especially as it becomes more widely known. This will happen whether you influence it or not. It is better to have a say in what your brand communicates to the market, rather than leave it to others to decide.

Understanding who it is you want to serve, what makes them tick, and why you are the best at meeting their needs enables you to:

* Focus on your values and purpose
* Target your marketing so that it specifically speaks to your customers' needs
* Develop products that they want, that stand out from the crowd
* Make strategic decisions about how to grow the business
* Attract employees who feel the same way

Employees. You want to attract the right employees to represent your brand, but how do you get people who are as good as you are with your customers?

Some businesses just seem to get recruitment right. Take John Lewis, Virgin, and Apple, for example. In an Apple store, you consistently get helped by staff who are great at solving customers' problems or helping them choose their next device. This is because Apple carefully chooses people who share the vision and values of the company and who believe in the brand. Brands attract people because of what they stand for, and that isn't any different when it comes to attracting employees instead of customers.

If you have a clear brand promise that outlines who you are and what you stand for, you will attract people who believe what you believe. This makes it easier to live up to the expectations of both your customers and employees. You minimise the chances of upsetting your customers if you have employees who think the same way. They become your advocates. They then set an expectation of the experience you will get, both as a customer and an employee, which strengthens the perception people have of your brand. It just makes sense.

People can be a company's biggest asset: a form of differentiation in a crowded marketplace. If you get the right people sitting in the right seats in your business, you will be a long way towards becoming a success.

Community. Community perception is sometimes overlooked, but it is extremely important. Community covers anyone who is not an employee or a customer, but is aware of your brand and therefore has an opinion about it. It could consist of your suppliers, partners, competitors or your prospects. They could be industry experts, media publications or journalists. At some stage, members of your community may become your customers or employees, or they could just be those who hear your story from someone who has experienced your brand. Either way, they will have an opinion, and how much they talk about you will depend on how strong that opinion is. And while you want them to talk about you, it should only be for the right reasons.

Breaking through as a brand is difficult. You have the industry market leaders to overturn and a reputation to build so you can compete with those corporate enterprises who dominate your sector. Reputations take years to form and minutes to ruin, so making sure you are influencing people in a positive way is crucial to the success of your brand. At the very worst you want people to have a neutral opinion of your brand, but actually you want your target customer avatars to shout from the rooftops about you. Who do your ideal customers and employees generally mix with socially? Probably other people just like them. If you are laser-focused on who you want your business to attract and have tailored your products or services towards them, they will tell other people they know about you, who might also be your target market. Whether those people are told a positive or a negative story is entirely up to you, but the story will be told whether you like it or not.

Providing a consistent brand experience, then, is crucial for gaining the right brand reputation. Is there any way to supply a consistent experience, or is it just a façade? Some brands get it right more often than not, but why don't more businesses get it right? There are lots of elements that need to be considered, but by following the Beyond Brand methodology they can be simplified into the seven easy principles that you can apply to your business model today. We'll cover these three audiences in further detail soon, as understanding your audiences is the second of our principles, but we suggest you start by forming what we call the brand promise.

Brand promise

'Making promises and keeping them is a great way to build a brand.'

Seth Godin

All good buildings that stand the test of time have firm foundations. A good brand isn't any different. If people cannot connect with your brand, then they judge you only on traditional values – product, price, availability. As soon as someone else is cheaper than you, builds a better product, or is more convenient, then customers are gone. In order to keep people attracted to your brand, you need to create something that resonates with them, something they can connect to.

A brand needs to have a personality, and at the core of that is your brand promise.

Your brand promise consists of six elements:

- Purpose
- Mission
- Vision
- Values
- Behaviours
- Goals

We'll go through each of them to explain the role they play in communicating to your audiences.

Purpose. The unifying principle that drives everything the organisation does. When brands are formed because of something they believe in, rather than just to make money, they channel all their energy into everything they do. That makes it easy to align everything else with the brand promise, because it is the guiding principle. Take Disney, for example. Disney's purpose is 'To create happiness through magical experiences'. From films to theme parks, cartoons to characters, everything that Disney does is based around that principle.

Mission. While your purpose is your guiding principle, your mission is the specific focus you are currently working towards, and it may shift as the market or environment changes over time. Unlike your purpose, it can change.

Take Apple as an example. Its purpose is well known to be 'Think different'. But Apple has applied this purpose to many missions. It has revolutionised the music industry with iTunes and the iPod by creating '1,000 songs in your pocket'. It has changed the way the telecommunications industry works by defining how smart the smartphone would be and how it could be purchased in a market that was previously dominated by the network providers.

As with Apple, your missions will change, but they enable you to be clear about where your business is currently heading. You may be revolutionising the definition of a product or taking your business global, fixing a problem no one else has fixed or implementing a transformational strategy.

Vision. Where you'll be when you've done it. Your vision describes how it will feel, what will be different and how your business will be known when you have reached your goals.

Creative geniuses, people like Steve Jobs and Elon Musk, are often described as being visionary. They can imagine a better world and can see the benefits of what it will be like when their ventures take you there. Sometimes your customers and employees will help take you closer to your vision and they will certainly be inspired by it if they commit to being with you for a prolonged period of time. It allows people to align with you, so paint a strong vision. Capture people's imagination and inspire them to become part of your brand's revolution.

Values. Your belief in how things should be done. Your moral compass. Values explain how you do things. They represent the key ethics of your brand's attitude and how it forms part of your brand's personality.

Each of us has a view about how people and businesses should conduct themselves. We judge a brand based upon its moral values and character. Does it have integrity? Can we trust it to have our best interests at heart? Does it show its values consistently in the way it behaves?

When you're choosing your company values, don't just look through the business dictionary for words that sound impressive. Values tie into your vision and purpose. They are your core beliefs and need to shine through in your culture, products and experience.

Brands like Squarespace show how values represent a company's every day approach. Check out Squarespace's website for some inspiration **https://www.squarespace.com/about/company/** to guide you to your own unique brand personality.

Get creative; think about what makes you different and what you stand for, then pull the themes together into easy-to-explain values that both your customers and employees can align with.

Behaviours. Behaviours are how you bring your values to life in every interaction, touch point and intention. They are the barometer by which your staff represent your brand.

When someone isn't behaving in the way you expect for your brand, they are often held up as 'not living the values'. By explaining your values fully, you can be clear what you expect of each individual. Have a manifesto for all employees to follow that connects the behaviour expected of them with your values and brand promise. If you tolerate bad behaviour, it becomes an option for your staff. You require strong leadership from the CEO down to each line manager, but we will talk about leadership later in the book.

Goals. These are measurable achievements that take you closer to fulfilling your vision, achieving your mission and bringing your purpose to life. They enable you to track your progress and demonstrate it to your team, stakeholders and customers. A moving set of objectives, these add up to the bigger goal or mission, so make sure you reset them once they are achieved.

All the elements of the brand promise are interconnected and are the foundations of your brand. Your brand promise is the heart and personality of the brand. It explains what you believe in and where you are going. It gives clarity and an anchor point. Always ask 'Does this fit our brand promise?' when you're faced with a decision for the brand. Whether that is what product to create, or what person to employ, the brand promise gives you a lens to look through when making important decisions.

Take time to create a strong brand promise. It will be time well spent, as you will be articulating to the world what you stand for.

What's the problem?

'People don't want to buy a quarter-inch drill, they want a quarter-inch hole.'

Theodore Levitt

The saying is true. You don't buy the drill because you want to own a drill. You buy the drill because you want the hole. But that's not really what you want either! Maybe you want to hang some shelves up in the garage. So, are you buying the ability to create shelves? No. The shelves enable you to store things neatly, freeing up the space. That's because you have just got a new bike and you need the space to store it.

What problem do you solve for your customers? Have you thought about it in this way when trying to show the value of what your business can give them? Henry Ford famously said, 'If I had asked people what they wanted, they would have said faster horses', and he was right. People often don't know what they want or need, but they do know what problems they need solving. In Henry Ford's case, his target customers knew that they wanted to get from A to B quicker.

People also know what dreams they'd like to achieve, but pain is usually a much bigger driver than gain. Do you know what your customers' pain is? Their specific problem? This is where you get right down into the differentiation. Sell the dream, tell the story, and create the emotion that the customers will feel when they work with you. Your customers need you to recognise their pain and show clearly how it will feel when your proposition has fixed it for them.

Do you know what their dreams are? Are there any trends in your target market? Are there micro-niches with specifics that you can own more than anyone else?

These are the questions you need to answer. Get into your customers' heads. Is it really a problem or just something that annoys them? What would they be able to do differently if I solved that for them? What would it feel like for them once they don't have to worry about that problem anymore? What could they be spending that time on, or what dreams could it enable them to realise?

Examples of pain versus gain points are below:

Pain	Gain
Increased cost of sale	Savings from operating costs
No time	More time
Image in the market	New customers queuing up
Losing sales	Recommendations from existing customers
Shrinking volumes	Growing book
Retention of customers	Loyalty of long-term custom

Stop asking what the market wants and start asking what your customers' pain and gain points are. Once you know what your customers' problems are, you can explore what makes you different and show why you are more than just a 'me too' brand.

Me too!

> *'In order to be irreplaceable, one must always be different.'*
>
> **Coco Chanel**

When you look at what your brand offers, is it any different to what anyone else is offering, or are you just another 'me too' brand? This may sound a bit harsh, but that could be the way your target market is looking at your business.

- Do you hold a position in the market that is uniquely yours?
- Are customers able to get the solution elsewhere?
- Do you solve a specific problem that no one else does?
- Do you do something in a way that no one else does?

If you cannot answer these questions with total conviction, then you are replaceable. As soon as someone comes along who can do it quicker, cheaper, better than you can, you will be history.

We call brands like these 'me too' brands.

In order to survive in your market over a period of time, you will need to have a USP: something that makes you different from the competition. Unless you are in a very niche market then the chances are that you will have a large pool of competition that customers can choose from. And unless customers are unhappy with their current providers, then convincing them to switch to you could be tricky. You may be cheaper than the competition, but that isn't sustainable unless you can deliver with reduced operating costs to preserve your margin. You may offer a slightly better product or service, but these days, that can be copied or improved on in weeks. Ultimately, if you are to take and retain a significant market share, then you need to provide an experience that is better than anything offered by your competitors today. It needs to be distinctly yours!

Think about what you can offer that is uniquely yours and hard to copy. Be honest with yourself about what it is that makes you different. You have to be able to prove the difference, otherwise it isn't real. It doesn't have to be a physical thing; it could be the way you make people feel when they interact with you. It could be a customer journey that is slicker than anyone else's.

Take Amazon, for example. Amazon is disrupting the market, pushing boundaries, and setting the standards that other retailers now have to live up to. You can set up an account in minutes and place an order that will be with you by tomorrow, or instantly if it is a digital product. They are leading the way, not following or chasing.

Brands that change the way we do business for the better, rather than just offering what everyone else does, are the ones that grow the quickest. They look beyond the way things have been done in the past and take market share quickly as a result of solving a frustration that customers had. For example, Moonpig, which launched in 2000, disrupted the industry of card shops by offering a service that would remember birthdays and special occasions for customers. It also offered personalised cards that people could design and send online without having to leave their computer. By 2007, Moonpig was responsible for 90% of the online card market in the UK, with over six million cards shipped.[3] The company made a seven-figure profit before being acquired by PhotoBox in 2011 for £120m.

DOLLAR SHAVE CLUB CASE STUDY

When Mark Levine and Michael Dubin founded Dollar Shave Club, their aim was simple: to ship low-cost razor blades straight to customers' homes for as little as $3 a month through a subscription service, drastically reducing the cost of shaving and successfully competing with market leaders. Genius. The company released a YouTube video in March 2012 called *Our Blades Are F***ing Great*,[4] which went viral, crashing its website in the first hour.

Dollar Shave Club built up a connection with its customers, through its engaging content and through communicating in a language customers found entertaining and easily consumable. In 2016, Unilever paid $1 billion for the company – about five times the revenue that Dollar Shave Club was expected to bring in that year.

---

3 https://en.wikipedia.org/wiki/Moonpig
4 https://youtu.be/ZUG9qYTJMsl

Being different attracts people who are looking for that difference. If you are not measured on the same 'me too' criteria as other brands in the market, you don't have to compete directly on product or price. Instead, you can create a niche following. Niche doesn't necessarily mean small; it just means you are creating a product for those who care about something specific. When you create something that is distinctly yours, it becomes what you are known for. It should flow through everything you do, the words you use, the content you produce, the purpose you stand for.

Start today. Think about why you are different, and if you realise that you are not, think about what you need to change to stand out.

 EXERCISE 1

- Brand promise – What is the definition of your brand promise? Create yours today by writing it out.

- USP – What is it that makes you distinctly different?

Getting emotional

According to Edelman, 87% of customers want a 'meaningful relationship with brands'.[5] Yet in a Havas Meaningful Brands Survey,[6] people also said they wouldn't care if 74% of brands fell off the face of the earth tomorrow.

So, what is the reality?

The competitive advantage has moved on from product or price. To have meaningful, long-term relationships with your customers, you have to build an emotional connection to your brand. Whether that emotion is one that people remember as being more personal, more efficient or even more fun, is down to your design. But if emotion doesn't come into the customer journey, then it just becomes a transaction. Transactions instead of relationships mean no loyalty. So how do you build that connection?

You need to know your audiences. What is your motive and intent for building a relationship with your target customers? Is it for you or for them? This is a crucial question. If your primary interest is your own success then you are building the relationship on rocky foundations. To build trust, you and your customers have to come to the table with the same intent and purpose.

---

5   https://www.edelman.com/news/consumers-view-relationships-brands-one-sided-limited-value/
6   http://www.meaningful-brands.com/en

BLOCKBUSTER VERSUS NETFLIX CASE STUDY

Blockbuster Video had no relationship with its customers, and this was the main reason for its demise. After being outraged at obtaining a $40 late fee for *Apollo 13*, Reed Hastings founded Netflix, where customers could pay a set fee each month with no late fees. Although previously enjoying annual revenues of over $5 billion, Blockbuster had lost its customers' trust with its business model, which was based on punishing people for the company's own gain. In 2000, the company earned $800 million in late fees alone, which accounted for 16% of its revenue. By 2002 Blockbuster posted losses of $1.6 billion. By 2010 the company was worth just $24 million, with $1.1 billion in revenue losses. Blockbuster eventually went bankrupt, while Netflix went on to be valued at over $100 billion in 2017.[7] In an ironic twist, Blockbuster had been given a chance to purchase Netflix for a mere $50 million, but had declined.[8] How different things could have been if Blockbuster had learned earlier that doing the right thing for your customers should be your number one rule.

7   https://www.topaccountingdegrees.org/netflix-vs-blockbuster/
8   http://www.businessinsider.com/how-netflix-bankrupted-and-destroyed-blockbuster-infographic-2011-3?IR=T

Smaller businesses have a real advantage over big corporate brands when it comes to creating an emotional connection with their customers. They have fewer customers, so can get to know them well. They can build relationships, be personal, and connect with people on a deeper level.

Keith, the coffee shop owner at my local train station, knows his customers by name, what's going on in their lives, and what they drink. He makes it his business to get to know them with a genuine intent, too. Not only does he serve great coffee, but he also starts people's day off with a welcoming personal conversation and a positive outlook on the day ahead. People remember that when they drink their coffee in the morning. Keith gets it.

There are many different forms of purpose which can connect with your customers, and next we will cover one specific type: social purpose.

Social purpose

Social purpose is the external benefit a business brings that society would miss if the business didn't exist. It is subtly different to corporate social responsibility, which supports the specific community a business may damage through its existence. Social purpose is the part of your business model that provides the best means to create a positive impact on society, by leveraging what the company is best at. It connects to your business purpose and your brand promise, and guides your business decisions in its future direction.

At Beyond Brand Group, our social purpose is 'Allowing everyone to have amazing experiences', and we do this in many different ways. We are committed to helping businesses of all sizes create amazing experiences for their customers and employees, thus enabling smaller businesses to thrive alongside the corporate giants. But our purpose also shines through in our support for our chosen charity, Molly Olly's Wishes, in a unique way. For every paying customer who works with us, we donate an experience to a terminally ill child. Whether that be a trip to a theme park, or a bedroom makeover, we give an experience to someone who needs one. By combining our purpose with our charitable beliefs, we are able to give back and show our customers and employees the difference they are making in society.

Because of the sensitive emotions you are connecting with, your social purpose needs to be sincere and authentic. Don't stand for something you don't really care about. Your social purpose should form part of your strategic direction, so it's important that they don't clash.

I tend to follow the three Fs when thinking about social purpose:

- It can't be forced
- It can't be a fad
- It can't be fake

But social purpose is most definitely a USP, so if you care about making a difference somewhere, formalise it. Get it built into your internal communications so that all your employees can see the difference they are working towards. Make it visible to your customers. When your social purpose achieves something great, talk about it, but make sure that it has been done with the right intentions, and is sincere and honest.

Campaigns can go wrong if they are positioned in a way that can be misread – even great companies with honest intentions have tripped up on this. Starbucks launched their 'Race Together' initiative to spark a national dialogue about race after Howard Schultz became disturbed by the riots following the killings of Michael Brown and Eric Garner. Starbucks encouraged its baristas to write 'Race Together' on the cups of coffee they served and also engage customers in conversations. It backfired badly. Critics called it a superficial gesture and the backlash exploded on social media.[9] Even though Starbucks had sincere intentions, customers did not associate their purpose with this prickly topic. Unless your purpose is race related, then this is an area best avoided altogether, as Starbucks found out, much to their peril.

Which brings us on to the next crucial part of your purpose: the importance of transparency.

---

9   https://www.fastcompany.com/3046890/the-inside-story-of-starbuckss-race-together-campaign-no-foam

Transparency

*'Purpose is not an add-on, it's not an initiative.
It is a culture change and it never finishes.'*

Antony Jenkins, Barclays CEO

Havas have tracked the business performance of brands that consistently ranked highly in its 'Meaningful Brand Index' for over ten years. [10] Its statistics show that brands that rank highly for meaningfulness outperform others in the market by 206%.

In 2017, the top ten looked like this:

1. Google
2. PayPal
3. WhatsApp
4. YouTube
5. Samsung
6. Mercedes-Benz
7. Nivea
8. Microsoft
9. Ikea
10. Lego

There's quite an eclectic mix of businesses within that list, with many different propositions from many different sectors. What do they all have in common?

Havas found that the brands that scored highly are the ones that make a material difference to people's lives across several important levels. They functionally improve their proposition in comparison with their competitors,

---

10 http://www.havasmedia.de/media/mb17_brochure_print_ready_final-min.pdf

demonstrating the personal benefits they make to people's lives and the collective communities that they connect to. Personal benefits could include making a customer's life easier, saving them time, or enabling them to spend more time doing what they love. Collective benefits, on the other hand, are ways in which you make things better for the community, the workforce, or society.

People want a brand that understands these needs and demonstrates that it cares about what they care about – brands that go beyond the product or service they provide create a meaningful relationship with us, and gain a greater share of our lives. If these brands make a positive, tangible impact on what matters to us and do so consistently, then they are rewarded with our trust.

Connection + transparency + consistency = trust

Consistency of delivery is vital to ensure that the clarity of your brand promise is protected as the message about what you stand for spreads. This needs to flow from your strategy, through your organisational structure in the company leadership behaviours. Be clear about the benefits that you deliver to people's wellbeing. Specifically look out for areas that don't match your purpose or brand promise and remove them from your business without delay, otherwise they will dilute the importance you place on your purpose. Measure progress through insights and feedback. Remember, what gets measured gets managed, and your brand reputation is at stake!

Finally, talk about the positive difference you make. Talk about it a lot.

Internal communication

'Communication leads to community, that is, to understanding, intimacy and mutual valuing.'

Rollo May

Get your communications right and people will understand your 'why', what makes you different and the elements of your brand promise. Get it wrong and you will confuse people and damage your brand value, losing any advocacy you may have had.

Let's start with how you manage the communication of your purpose internally.

You have to communicate your purpose to everyone in your company, and this communication has to come from the top down. Make your brand promise the anchor point in the organisation to ensure it is seen as important and not just a fad. This promise will become a part of the culture of your business, so it is important to embed it into all internal communication channels. It should form part of your recruitment policy, be visible in people's behaviours, and flow through your operations from cradle to grave. This set of principles sets the expectations for your brand culture. Therefore:

* Celebrate people living up to the brand promise with their actions

* Deliver incentives that reward examples of purposeful behaviours

* Make it part of your performance review and your key performance indicators (KPIs)

Remember, consistency is key, so make it a measure of your progress. Make sure that your internal governance and approval processes are strong, and trust your gut.

External communication

'If I was down to the last dollar of my marketing budget, I would spend it on PR.'

Bill Gates

How well defined is your brand promise? If you asked your employees, customers, suppliers, or competitors, could they explain it clearly?

The clarity with which you communicate your message externally will directly correlate to the success you will have at attracting those who share your passion. It must be consistent across all channels, be they social, digital, traditional, white mail, advertising, or documents. It is important to avoid conflicting initiatives and stories, otherwise there will be confusion about what you actually stand for.

Let's take a look at a good example of the way a brand promise is communicated.

BMW 'THE ULTIMATE DRIVING MACHINE' CASE STUDY

Whenever BMW introduces a new model, the designers and engineers know their brief. Salespeople know how the car will be differentiated and customers know what to expect when they are looking to buy one. With 90% of the guesswork removed, customers can confidently buy the car without even seeing it first.

Knowing this, BMW has recently introduced a virtual showroom which allows customers to build their car online, view it, pay for it, and order it without even stepping inside a dealership. With the developments of virtual reality, a customer can enjoy that part of the experience without even leaving the comfort of their own home, giving BMW competitive advantage and stronger control, and delivering a very different customer experience.

Providing proof of its impact is crucial to keeping the brand promise alive. Marketing needs to 'feel right', and so do the PR communications that go out alongside the company results. Listening to and engaging with your audience will prevent you veering off track. The main goal is to retain the confidence of your target market and your employees too. So, let's take a look at both of those areas next, starting with customer confidence.

Customer confidence

> *'It takes twenty years to build a reputation and five minutes to ruin it. If you think about that, you'll do things differently.'*
>
> **Warren Buffett**

Customers will instantly recognise your brand if they remember the experience they had with you, so you want that to be a positive experience. The more often you deliver that, the more you will build their confidence. Servicing the customer must be evident across all the channels, media and touch points that they go through, as well as in your new product development. Don't just bolt the experience part on to the end.

Lots of brands have examples of getting it wrong, though. While they are not alone, BiC have twice fallen foul with their approach to reaching out to their female consumers. First, back in 2012, they created a real stir with the introduction of their 'BiC for Her' pens in 'pretty pink'. They were lambasted for the introduction of the product, with Innocent Drinks really taking advantage of the topic on social media and some comic reviews on Amazon creating even more negativity, all of which went viral.[11]

You would have thought that they had learned from this faux pas. But they then released a second shocking example on International Women's Day in 2015, which was supposed to be aimed at 'empowering women' but gained yet further media attention and some scathing brand damage. The

---

11   https://dailym.ai/2l41RhG

advert released by BiC South Africa featured a picture of a woman accompanied by four lines of text that said 'Look like a girl, act like a lady, think like a man, work like a boss'. Yet again BiC were in the news for all the wrong reasons, as they alienated half of the population in one fell swoop.[12]

---

12 https://www.prweek.com/article/1359651/bic-pens-two-apologies-sexist-blunder-when-promoting-national-womens-day

Employee engagement

'Appreciate everything your associates do for the business. Nothing else can quite substitute for a few well-chosen, well-timed, sincere words of praise. They're absolutely free and worth a fortune.'

Sam Walton, CEO and founder of Walmart

Most leaders would love to believe that their employees care just as much as they do about the brand, but that isn't always the case. Some brands do manage this, though, so what is it they do that is so different? Let's look at how engagement plays a key role in connecting with your audiences.

What works?

Your brand promise gives you a framework to base your whole employee experience on so that your internal culture matches the experience you want to deliver externally. It starts with your recruitment process. Employee behaviour should match your brand promise, so test that your expectations are met at all stages of the employee lifeline. Check at the recruitment stage, during employees' induction training, throughout their ongoing development, and at appraisal time.

Your culture must be apparent across all departments in your business, including among the leaders, who should demonstrate the consistency of the brand promise in the leadership of their teams. Empower people to hold each other accountable to the brand promise and challenge anything that doesn't feel in line with expectations. Map out the employee experience with the purpose and brand promise front of mind. If something doesn't feel like it delivers the brand promise, whether it is a process that drives the wrong outcome or an individual who displays the wrong behaviours, change it. Never compromise on the standards and expectations that you have set out in your brand promise. The minute you do, your brand promise will be seen as optional rather than compulsory.

For employees to deliver a great customer experience, they must first have a great employee experience. Engaged and energetic employees will love the brand as much as the customer, so measure and reward employee performance against brand promise metrics to demonstrate your commitment to its importance. Employee engagement is critical to your success, so it deserves to be held in as high regard as sales or service performance.

GETTING IT RIGHT – INCHCAPE CASE STUDY

In 2016, Inchcape was voted 'The No1 best big company to work for' in the *Sunday Times* Top 30, beating brands such as Santander and Nationwide. Inchcape tests how its employees view the company and uses these insights to set priorities for the following year. As results improve each year, Inchcape's profits, financial performance, and employee engagement also rise alongside them.

The reputation is viral!

Bad news stories travel quickly, but it isn't always customers or journalists spreading the news. It may be your employees.

Good quality employees have more choice than ever before. If you want the best, you have to compete. In the same way that they trust reviews on products and services, people trust the views of employees or ex-employees when they're considering which company to work for. Online forums such as Glassdoor and Trustpilot provide a platform for employees to rate and write detailed reviews of their employer.[13] [14] There are also lists such as the *Sunday Times* Top 100 for potential employees to consult.[15] Using these services, you can benchmark how your company ranks against others in your industry, as well as in the wider market.

Before we move on to the second principle of the Beyond Brand methodology, please take a moment to complete the exercise below.

---

13 https://www.glassdoor.co.uk
14 https://www.trustpilot.com
15 https://appointments.thetimes.co.uk/article/best100companies/

EXERCISE 2

The three Cs are crucial to the success of creating a culture which supports your brand promise and purpose:

- ❖ Connecting with your audiences
- ❖ Communication that reflects your unique brand promise
- ❖ Consistency in the way it is delivered

Rank how strong you are on these three key elements on a scale of one to seven, then consider where you would like to be. How wide is the gap? What will you need to stop, start or continue to get you to where you want to be?

Get started today. Your competitors probably already have.

Principle Two

AUDIENCES

Employees

> *'Clients do not come first. Employees come first. If you take care of your employees, they will take care of the clients.'*
>
> **Richard Branson**

If your employees are not engaged and enjoying an amazing employee experience, then you have little chance of fulfilling your brand promise. Therefore, they are the first audience you need to focus on. Having a solid people strategy is paramount to delivering a successful brand experience.

More than ever before, employees want to be associated with brands that care about the things they care about. They want to be treated as individuals and work in an environment that enables them to thrive. The best employees are looking for:

- Flexible working hours
- Choice of working environment
- Varied work experience
- Role diversity
- Opportunities for rapid progression into senior roles

Employees play a significant role in the future of the business. Consider the employee experience as a critical part of your brand success, and shape a proposition that attracts the kind of people you want in your business. Your recruitment campaigns need to inspire, stand out, and be different. Get creative and inspire your ideal employee to apply. For example, OgilvyOne's 2010 quest to find the world's greatest salesperson used a social media campaign to generate interest from far and wide.[16] All entrants had to do was submit a video demonstrating how they would go about selling a red brick.

If you get the experience right, then you will attract the right talent for your business. Create candidate personas of your existing most valuable employees (MVEs), to capture what it is about them that fits your business so well. 'Hire for will, train the skill' is one of the best pieces of advice you can follow, unless you need a certain skill standard in your industry. The best-qualified person in the world can kill your business if they have the wrong attitude and behaviours.

Take your time to recruit, but fire quickly. According to a report by Oxford Economics, the average cost of a bad hire comes out at over £30,000,[17] and that is before you consider any impact on brand reputation, client experience, customer impact etc.

Here are my top tips for successful recruitment:

1. Implement a probationary period to decide whether the recruit is absolutely right for the business.

2. The Six Ss. Support, support, support, support, support, sack. Identify any areas your recruit is falling down on and take action to help them. If they still don't come up to standard, do the right thing and cut the cord.

---

16   https://youtu.be/edZpR_Qd8rk.
17   http://www.hrreview.co.uk/hr-news/recruitment/it-costs-over-30k-to-replace-a-staff-member/50677

3. Protect MVEs. The most valuable employees are the ones you want to keep. Create bespoke plans that keep your best people with you for the long term. These could include role development, long-term incentive programmes, or even shares in the business. Make them a priority before it's too late.

4. Ensure you have a great career website. This is your opportunity to stand out from the competition and showcase the differences your employee experience brings. Use examples that attract the right people to your recruitment campaigns, bringing to life the culture and working environment they can expect when they work for you. Check out https://www. spotifyjobs.com or https://www.apple.com/jobs/uk/retail. html for some great examples of how to do this.

Invest in people

'It goes without saying that no company, small or large, can win over the long run without energized employees who believe in the mission and understand how to achieve it.'

Jack Welch, former CEO of General Electric

When you've recruited the right people, how do you keep them? There is a famous business joke involving a CFO who says, 'What if we train them and they leave?', only for the CEO to respond with, 'What if we don't and they stay?' Investing in people must be part of your ethos. You need to invest in people so that they can offer the best services to your clients. It forms the basis of the service–profit chain that was introduced to us by James L. Heskett, W. Earl Sasser and Leonard Schlesinger in 1994, and still rings true today.

Create a fantastic working environment, employ great people, and then keep them happy. They will deliver high-quality outputs to your customers, which will make customers loyal to your business. Repeat business and customer retention increase your revenues, profits, and customer base with referrals from satisfied customers.

It is less of a cost and more of an investment. Let's consider the benefits of investing in your MVEs:

- Reduced induction costs
- Increased efficiency benefit
- Lower rework figures
- Improved customer satisfaction
- Improved employee retention

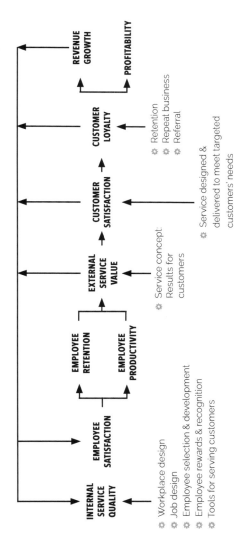

What things should you invest in to get the most bang for your buck? One way to ensure you get a balanced employee experience is to apply the ASK model, which measures their **a**ttitude, **s**kills, and **k**nowledge, and can be easily incorporated into your competency framework. This provides a clear outline of what you expect at each level from all employees, in terms of both behaviour and performance, against which to measure what makes a good employee.

An employee's development comes in many different formats, and structured courses should take up approximately 10% of their time. Other development resources include books, audio and e-learning, mentorship, and communities, which can be accessed both internally and externally from your business. Invest in a good leadership development programme too, if you want to keep the best assets you have.

Think ahead about how your people strategy will change as your business grows. Invest in personal development plans that grow the leadership skills within your team, so that employees can reach their potential. Develop a succession plan, identifying people for positions in your business as the growth happens. The Nine Box Planning Model is a useful tool to see where your people are today, identifying whom to invest in and how far they are from their next move.

Investing in people keeps them motivated. But whose job is it motivate the employees? In the next section, we'll explore how everyone plays a part in keeping motivation high among your employees, so that they can deliver the best results while gaining satisfaction in their roles.

9 BOX PLANNING

"Rough Diamond" Low Performer/ High Potential	**"Future Star"** Moderate Performer/ High Potential	**"Consistent Star"** High Performer/ High Potential
"Inconsistent Player" Low Performer/ Moderate Potential	**"Key Player"** Moderate Performer/ Moderate Potential	**"Current Star"** High Performer/ Moderate Potential
"Talent Risk" Low Performer/ Low Potential	**"Solid Professional"** Moderate Performer/ Low Potential	**"High Professional"** High Performer/ Low Potential

Potential Assessment ←

Performance Assessment →

Motivating matters

'The mediocre teacher tells. The good teacher explains. The superior teacher demonstrates. The great teacher inspires.'

William Arthur Ward

Whose job is it to motivate the employees in your business? The leaders'? The CEO's? Or do the employees motivate themselves? Leaders play a key role, but the truth is that it is the responsibility of everyone to create the right environment and culture, in which motivation is present at all points.

Motivation will be different for each individual, but there are common reasons why employees choose to leave one business to join another. Here are the top ten:[18]

1. Bad relationship with their boss
2. Bored and unchallenged by the work
3. Bad relationship with co-workers
4. Lack of opportunities to use skills and abilities
5. Lack of contribution of work to the organisation's business goals
6. Lack of autonomy and independence
7. Lack of meaningful work
8. Organisation's financial stability
9. Overall corporate culture

---

18 https://www.thebalance.com/top-reasons-why-employees-quit-their-job-1918985

10. Management's lack of recognition of the employee's job performance

Which ones can you eradicate or influence?

Warren Bennis said 'Leadership is the capacity to translate vision into reality' and he was right. Strong leadership gets the most out of your employees. A good leader provides employees with a career path, not just a job. They value employees, develop them, stretch them, and encourage them to work well together, to be the best they can be. This creates a fantastic working environment and company culture. Leaders find wins, not just problems.

So, what else?

It's important that you invest in the right people. Base your recruitment on finding people who share the same ethos as you. You and your leaders are removing the top ten reasons above and creating jobs that people love, in a company they want to be with.

Get to know your employees well. Use tools such as employee Net Promoter Score (eNPS) surveys, annual employee surveys, coffee and cake sessions, or walking the floor to listen to suggestions and explore improvements you can make in the business. Your employees are the most important asset you have. Do not underestimate the impact that spending time with them can have.

Make sure you reinforce the brand promise through your pay and rewards structure. Pay rates and benefits should be driven by the right behaviours and considered across all levels in your organisation, not just for the sales teams.

This will help to keep the top talent within your business, so make sure you give it the attention it deserves.

What other incentives do employees care about? These are the top five benefits ranked by employees in a recent study by Glassdoor:[19]

1. Healthcare insurance (40%)
2. Paid time off (37%)
3. Performance bonus (35%)
4. Paid sick days (32%)
5. Retirement plan/pension (31%)

A salary and benefits package that is competitive in your market will attract great talent, but what else could you offer? For example, Facebook gives its employees $4,000 of 'baby cash' when they have a newborn. If you want your employees to be loyal and feel valued, you need to offer good all-round packages.

---

19 https://www.glassdoor.com/blog/ecs-q3-2015/

Who owns the customer?

'If you are not serving the customer, your job is to be serving someone who is.'

Jan Carlson

Whose responsibility is it to ensure that your customers get the experience you intend for them? The biggest difference between organisations that are truly customer-centric and those that aren't is whether they are integrated or run in departmental silos. A great customer experience is down to how joined up your departments are and the information that flows between them.

Pulling departments together can be tricky. What you want is a culture that puts the best interests of the customer front and centre of every decision you make. Therefore, the customer plays a part in everybody's role, but this must start from the very top of the business. Whatever the size of your business, if the CEO and the top table are not aligned on this, then it won't be ingrained in the culture of the business. Leaders play a key role in ensuring that the company strategy cascades down from the CEO, making its way into the objectives, goals, behaviours, and targets of every role, holding everyone accountable. It is then a case of providing employees with freedom within a framework to deliver the company strategy in a way that meets the brand promise.

But who do you want to reach with this message? Who are the perfect customers for whom you are the only brand? Let's explore how to find the second audience for your brand, your customers.

The perfect customer

'Don't find customers for your products, find products for your customers.'

Seth Godin

Your customers will need to connect and resonate with your brand if you are to have any chance of leading your market, but you only need the customers you want to attract. If you try to appeal to everyone, you will actually specialise in no one. Therefore, you will make no one feel special.

You may have a number of different customer types in your customer mix, so gather as much information as possible about the traits of your customer personas (or avatars). How old are they? What percentage are male versus female? What do they value? Where do they hang out? The more you know about your customers, the easier it will be to develop your products and services to meet their wants and needs. To help you, download my checklist http://www.beyondbrand.org/bbmtemplates/ and start building your customer personas.

This will help you understand your best customers better. Best customers? Surely all customers are treated the same way and we value them all? We absolutely do care about all customers who choose to use our brand in their lives. However, I have a little secret for you... Not all customers are equal. Some customers are more valuable and important to your business than others.

Let's look at an example. You are a customer of a well-respected supermarket. You spend around £200 per week there, and have been doing so for the last five years, but at Christmas you didn't manage to get your turkey there. Turkeys had sold out – bought up by non-regular customers who had only come to that supermarket because they'd heard it had great turkeys in stock. Now you have to go somewhere else for your Christmas turkey.

Would you have felt like a valued customer? Would you expect to be treated a little differently? Of course, you'd have every right to, as you provide a far greater value to the business than the once-a-year shopper. The business should know this and be prepared to do something special to protect those customers who are loyal and have a high lifetime value. It could offer a special Christmas hamper for its regulars, or a gold customer evening with exclusive use of the store after hours. Service differentiation isn't a bad thing, so long as everyone gets an acceptable standard of service to start with.

It's good to define exactly whom you are trying to please, and who your least valuable customers are. The cost of sale and the cost to serve can vary dramatically between your various different audiences, so it is important to establish the amount of profit you will get for the amount of effort you need to put in. Let go of the customers who are not right for your brand. Recommend another company to them, then invest your efforts in the customers who give you a strong lifetime value.

Use the methods we have described above to ensure you focus on those who are your best customers. Stick to your brand promise and you will build a tribe of people who believe what you stand for and like the way it differentiates you from the competition.

Why me?

'Get closer than ever to your customers. So close that you tell them what they need well before they realize it themselves.'

Steve Jobs

Why do your customers choose you over your competition? Some may prefer your website, the quality of your paperwork, or the way you make it so easy to order. Knowing their reasons enables you to focus on and manage the areas that matter to them, tailoring your marketing to deliver a better conversion rate from your advertising and direct contact. Build a picture of how and why you add value to your customers' lives and show why your proposition will feel different to the other options they have to choose from. In essence, make it easy for them to choose you.

Even if you have ultra-niche, high-end clientele, the one thing they can't buy is more time. Being able to experience life to its fullest is becoming more important than ever. Therefore, having time to do the things we love provides us with something priceless. The world is evolving to make customers' lives easier, and those who succeed in enabling this are winning.

Ten years ago, we didn't have TV on demand. Now music, TV, and video are streamed instantly. Personalised content is recommended to us so we don't even have to find it. Various digital solutions learn our likes, removing the hassle. It doesn't matter if it's not that slick behind the scenes; as far as the customer is aware, the new world is providing perfect solutions that appear instantly.

Loyalty can compete, but only for so long. This is even more reason for you to prioritise building relationships as part of your customer retention strategy. The experience is what they will remember and tell their friends about, so make sure it is memorable and personal rather than transactional. Being more nimble and agile, smaller businesses can change their processes to keep up with customer expectations. Larger corporates have a big tanker to turn; changes take them time to implement and even longer to get right consistently.

Consistency delivers the expectation of what you will get from interacting with a brand. It becomes the brand. It becomes what people share with others, influencing their opinions about your brand. And influencers can be extremely powerful in growing your reputation. In the next section, let's look at the importance of getting this right by looking at the third audience, which we call 'community'.

The influencers

'Your brand is what other people say about you when you're not in the room.'

Jeff Bezos

There is a big world out there that has an opinion about your brand. They may not be customers or employees now, but they may be soon. They may talk about your brand, dream in front of your shop window, or recommend you to someone who is a perfect fit for your customer persona.

These people are your community. They could be friends of customers, people you meet in the pub, ex-employees, or even your competitors. They know your brand and have an opinion about it. What's important is that they talk about your brand for the right reasons.

You want your brand to have social appreciation – an acceptance of it being a good thing to have around. Maybe it solves a problem that no one else solves, or it may have aspirational qualities that people desire. Brands getting this right include Lego, IKEA and Nike. They spark positive emotions when people think of them; they have built that emotional connection to good memories.

What is the true power of getting influencers talking about your brand in a positive way though? How much can it affect your bottom line? Let's look at the power of recommendations.

Power of recommendations

'Nothing influences people more than a recommendation from a trusted friend.'

Mark Zuckerberg

Today, 88% of customers are influenced by online review ratings of customer service when making a purchase. As 95% of customers share bad experiences, you can really damage your brand reputation if you get it wrong.

It isn't all bad news, though, as 87% of customers tell people when they have a good experience.[20] Social proof, then, plays a big part in our purchasing decisions and we now trust the reviews of total strangers online above the advice given to us by any retailer.

Your reputation goes viral almost instantly if the news is interesting or scandalous enough. Media and profiling are so highly sharable now that you need care and attention to ensure your brand perception remains in line with your brand promise. The consistency with which this is applied shows your audiences why your brand differs from others.

Next we'll look at how you can engage your audiences further, but before that, please take a moment to complete the following exercise.

---

20 https://www.zendesk.com/resources/customer-service-and-lifetime-customer-value/

EXERCISE 3

- Who are your MVCs (most valuable customers)? What makes up their personas? What margins do they give you? What mix do you have in your customer groups? What are your customer target markets?

- Who are your MVEs (most valuable employees)? What makes up their personas, behaviours and values?

- How does your brand promise match to your MVPs' (most valuable people) personas?

Trust and influence

'If you don't have trust inside your company, then you can't transfer it to your customers.'

Roger Staubach

Trust is built up over a long time, but it can be accelerated by the views of others or by events that have a positive emotional impact on you. Trust is maintained by many small actions, consistently delivered over time. When customers trust a person or a brand, they have committed emotionally and are willing to be influenced by the brand's personality.

Emotional connection + trust = influence

Without trust and an emotional relationship, we make decisions based on the views of others, social proof, reviews, or endorsements from people we do trust. Loyalty and advocacy only come when someone feels you have their best interests at heart, otherwise all you have is a transactional relationship.

To build a loyal following, you have to be transparent about what you want to do as a brand, and receptive to the views of the people you want to be part of it. Trusted brands forge connections to build a community where they interact with open, two-way communication over various channels.

Don't try to sell products to first-time customers with a scattergun approach; take the time to get to know them first. You wouldn't ask a person to marry you on the first date, so why do some companies use exactly that approach when selling to prospective customers? Send them content that will entertain or educate them. Be cool and fun with your customers, matching your communication style to the customer personas you have built up from your data. It will pay off in the long term.

Dove, Fisher Price, and Johnson & Johnson are all examples of companies that trigger a sense of trust and influence from a brand that has built a connection with its customers. If you are to build that kind of brand connection, you need to ensure that the customer experience is consistent across all the touch points in your business. This means you will need to trust and empower others to deliver the experience you have designed.

Empowering

> 'An empowered organization is one in which individuals have the knowledge, skill, desire, and opportunity to personally succeed in a way that leads to collective organizational success.'
>
> **Stephen Covey**

Trust relies on empowerment to enable your employees to 'do the right thing'. They need 'freedom within a framework' to enable them to translate the ethos of your brand promise into practice. This may mean bending the rules; it may mean giving them financial responsibility or time to commit to future projects. You need to give them the same trust that you are looking to get from your customers.

Create an environment that allows your employees to work in this way. Determine the roles that they play, as well as the rules and boundaries that allow them to thrive within your risk tolerances. Where possible, do this with your employees. If you explain your expectations and framework plainly, with a clearly defined brand promise, then most employees will know instinctively what to do. Make sure your approach is fully understood and consistent across the business.

John Lewis doesn't have employees, it has partners. And while they may do this through mutual ownership in the business, this is exactly the approach all businesses can take to shift their thinking. Recognise the role your employees have in making your business better, stronger, and more successful in your industry. Commit to a shift in the way that you work. Place your trust in your team without wavering. Approach your goals together; to get everyone engaged.

Let's get engaged

'When people are financially invested, they want a return. When people are emotionally invested, they want to contribute.'

Simon Sinek

'Engagement' is a word often preceded by 'employee', but great companies also get engaged with their customers and their community. Engagement requires shared values and respect, an expectation of what good behaviours look like, and a desire to look after each other's best interests. It requires commitment, loyalty and trust. It has to be earned and cannot be bought.

Employee engagement helps employees to see the difference they can make to the future of the company. Just recruiting great people is not enough to keep them.

How can you retain employee engagement over the longer term? Think about developing career pathways and succession planning. Allow employees to get involved in activities that give them wider fulfilment on top of their day jobs. Broaden their knowledge and skills by involving them in projects that challenge them outside of their current role.

Today's workers want a good work–life balance, and experiences are part of their life goals. They may want to be around for their children's key moments or to travel the world. Flexible working environments enable them to realise their goals.

A key part of work–life balance is your employees' health and wellbeing. Make sure they are healthy and fit; make it easy for them to eat good food; be supportive of exercise programmes and health-scanning – these are just some of the things that businesses can do to provide caring options for their employees. With people living longer, they are also working further into their later years. Taking care of your employees can reduce absence levels and also help them stay healthy for longer.

While a good financial package is important to employees, recognition is also powerful. Embed rewards and recognition schemes into your structures to show employees that you appreciate their efforts. Sometimes a sincere and honest 'well done' can be good enough. Praise can be a huge motivator. Most of all, the journey you are on together should be fun.

Understanding what makes your target audiences tick and tailoring your messages to meet their needs will go a long way towards building crucial relationships. Listen to what they have to say about your brand and their expectations of you using surveys, interviews, focus groups, coffee and cake sessions, group huddles, or Monday motivation briefs. It needs to be a 360° feedback loop, with all parties being informed about the progress you've made as a result of the feedback they have given. The only thing worse than not asking for feedback is asking for it then doing nothing with it.

Sounds like a lot of effort. Surely as the business leader you already know what direction you need to be heading in. So what more can customers add and is it worth all this extra effort?

What do they know?

'Most people do not listen with the intent to understand; they listen with the intent to reply.'

Stephen Covey

Your audience has a lot of the answers to the problems and challenges that you face, if you bother to ask them. They can help you structure improvements, make good use of your investments in developments and accelerate your progress. It's about creating the right environment where your audiences can share ownership for the development of your proposition. Access to the CEO and key members of the senior team is really powerful. When audiences are brutally honest about their experiences, it can be a big realisation exercise for business leaders.

Customers should feel valued, accepted and respected. Therefore, update them on the progress you've made since they gave you their feedback in the same way you would your employees. Explain if you are not going to do anything with certain elements of their feedback, and why you have arrived at that decision.

Finally, make sure you listen to the right people. Listening to the wrong people could end up taking you in a direction that is further away from those you are trying to connect with. You need an effective way of filtering out all the wrong information to give you a pure view of your direction, but don't throw any information away, as it may hold nuggets for the future. You can easily burn through a whole load of cash and time if you are guessing how to improve rather than asking. Don't allow yourself to get distracted from what is really important. So, get creative. Build flexibility into your approach and be imaginative, so that people can choose a style of giving feedback that works for them. When this feedback process works well, you can capture some fantastic ideas to keep your loyal customers and stakeholders on board.

Who wants it?

'Some stakeholders are completely behind the project, so they can stab it in the back.'

Anon

If you are going to get behind your new culture, you need to ensure that it has the support of the biggest influencers in the business. If your key stakeholders are not really behind it, your new culture will fail. For a universal shift to happen, it needs to be built into the business right from the top. And that starts with the business owner or CEO. Address any concerns that senior leaders may have and you will have a much smoother ride. This is crucial to the long-term success of your programme implementation. Be aware of the politics going on around you to make it easier for you to bring people back on track. And if you are the most senior leader in the business, you need to be an active supporter of new cultures, removing any barriers.

A CEO engaged in a brand experience programme will provide platforms such as blog posts, monthly updates, conferences, or meetings to communicate changes to the rest of the business and allow employees at every level to speak about the changes. Employees' support will help the changes flow through the organisation at a much faster rate and with more gravitas too.

Programmes and changes can take a long time to implement, depending on the size of your business, so put milestones in place when you can update people on progress and celebrate successes along the way. Make time for it as a key deliverable, tying it all back to the brand promise and the overarching reason that the company exists.

Different people will want to engage on different levels. Some will be comfortable with the changes, others will want to ask questions. Some may be nervous about what the changes will mean to them and the business, so make sure you consider the different generations and personality types in your business.

The generation game

> *'If you want to make everyone happy, don't be a leader, sell ice cream.'*

Steve Jobs

How do you create a business that is cutting edge and innovative, but doesn't alienate the different generations of your audience?

Audiences are changing significantly in their expectations. Baby Boomers are in the workspace now, but are coming to the end of their careers. Generation X are in their senior years of working, while Millennials, who make up the largest segment of today's audiences, are heading into their late thirties. A new generation, known as Generation Z, is now entering the workforce and they are becoming consumers. Each generation has different priorities and motivators.

Boomers are hard-working, self-centred people who have focused on their careers and built for retirement. They are the first generation where both parents typically worked full time, growing their careers through the hierarchy structure, predominantly with one or two companies, before retiring.

Generation X grew up with Boomer parents, so they are used to being independent, optimistic and freethinking. They have come through the introduction of the internet and computers. Their careers have been more about themselves than the company, and therefore they have moved from one company to another more freely. They also have a bigger pull towards brands and labels than previous generations.

The Millennials grew up digitally native, never remembering a time without computers. They socialise via devices and schedule everything in their busy lives. They work to live rather than live to work, and they prefer to spend their money on experiences rather than owning lavish goods. Nine out of ten Millennials would switch brands to support a particular cause, and 87% would purchase a product with a social or environmental benefit.[21]

Generation Z are the streaming generation, expecting instant availability. They play with toys for less time than previous generations, using technology to gain their pleasures. Because of this, they have gained the tag of KGOY (kids growing older younger) as they discard traditional toys for modern digital options. They are used to being hammered by brands with advertising, turning them into savvy consumers who do not suffer fools easily.

How can you appeal to everyone? We are in a period of moving from traditional generations to the new digital eras, with some significant shifts in personality and values. This is where the work you have done on understanding your purpose, brand promise, and audience personas will come into its own. Instead of trying to appeal to all the generations, consider what it is about your company that makes you different to the competition. Your purpose and brand promise may appeal to several generations as demographics and personas start to add colour to who your perfect audience is. You may be a fitness company that specialises in time-poor, cash-rich individuals, or you may

---

21 http://www.conecomm.com/research-blog/2015-cone-communications-millennial-csr-study

run a cloud storage business that makes it easier to pull together online storage for technophobes. It doesn't need to be about the generation; it's about your solution being better for a specific group of individuals who get what it is you do and what you stand for. It's about your brand being better to work for than other employers, because you understand your ideal employees and have matched the working environment and package to suit their needs.

Solutions can exist across generations; you just need to make sure that you have considered which communication approaches and channels your audiences expect from the brands they choose. We will explore how to use channels to your advantage later in the book, but before that, we'll move into the third principle of the Beyond Brand methodology: the approach you use to reach your audiences.

But first, please take some time to complete the exercise below to consider how you are engaging and empowering your audiences.

EXERCISE 4

- Think of the methods you use today to engage your customer and employee audiences. Are there new ones you could add or ways you could improve on your current approaches?

- Consider the power of social proof and story-telling. How do you use them in your business? What stories could you use to harness your potential even further?

- Explore what empowerment opportunities you could put in place to make your employees feel like they are contributing to the improvement of the brand experience.

- Consider which 'listen and learn' activities you could add into your business to connect more often with your perfect audiences.

Principle Three

APPROACH

Experience as a strategy

'Whatever you do, do it well. Do it so well that when people see you do it they will want to come back and see you do it again, and they will want to bring others and show them how well you do what you do.'

Walt Disney

Do you leave your brand experience to chance, or have you strategically planned how it will be delivered consistently every time? By 2020, customer experience will overtake price and product as the key brand differentiator. It is the new area where competitive advantage can be seized. Customer experience needs to be personal, it should feel different, and it needs to be delivered consistently.

Businesses are slowly realising they need to be leading the pack in terms of customer experience, otherwise a competitor will make this a priority and replace them. Gartner predicted that by 2016, 89% of companies would be competing primarily on the basis of customer experience.[22] While 95% of the C-Suite (the chief officers in a company) have accepted that customer experience needs to be one of the top three priorities, only about 37% of companies have an active strategy to improve it.[23] It seems some business leaders don't know where to start, while others don't know if the return on investment (ROI) will pay

---

22 https://www.gartner.com/smarterwithgartner/customer-experience-battlefield/

23 https://brpconsulting.com/within-5-years-75-of-retailers-plan-to-identify-customers-when-they-walk-in-the-store/

off. Some smaller businesses I speak with haven't even heard the terms 'customer experience' or 'brand experience', often confusing them with customer service, branding, or marketing. Asking them whether they want to create advocacy or brand loyalty mostly doesn't get people's attention. Ask them if they want to attract and retain more customers, and all business leaders are interested. Add in that you can increase profit margins, reduce operating costs, and grow market share, and the conversation changes dramatically.

Competition for budget, though, is very competitive. Customer experience has to compete for investment against new product development, new IT systems and marketing budgets. We used to struggle to get the attention of the decision makers, but that is all changing now as companies realise that the experience is what sets them apart from the competition. Check out some of the ROI facts below:

- ❀ Companies that offer great customer experience have 2.5 times the number of engaged employees than those that don't[24]

- ❀ 82% of customers stopped doing business with a company after a bad experience[12]

- ❀ 86% of customers will pay up to 25% more for a good customer experience[25]

---

24 https://experiencematters.blog/engage-employees-great-cx-starts-with-engaged-employees/

25 https://www.slideshare.net/RightNow/2011-customer-experience-impact-report

- ❂ A 2% increase in customer retention can give you a 10% reduction in operating costs[26]

- ❂ When you offer a personalised customer experience, sales conversions increase by up to 14%[27]

Visit http://www.beyondbrand.org/roi/ to access a simple calculator that I have created to check how customer experience translates into financials.

Understanding what makes a business sustainable in today's landscape is essential. Markets have changed dramatically; some of today's market leaders didn't even exist ten years ago. If your competitive advantage comes from your brand experience, are your KPIs and business strategies aligned to your brand promise? How does your brand experience programme fit in with the rest of your ambitions for the business?

Let's explore the importance of aligning your strategies throughout the business plan.

---

26 E.C. Murphy and M. A. Murphy (2002), *Leading on the Edge of Chaos: The 10 Critical Elements for Success in Volatile Times*, Upper Saddle River, NJ: Prentice Hall

27 http://www.aberdeen.com/research/7635/ra-social-media-marketing/content.aspx

Aligning strategies

'Building a visionary company requires one percent vision and 99 percent alignment.'

Jim Collins

Does the customer sit at the centre of all your decisions, or do you start from a product or profit perspective? Your strategies should all be driven by your brand promise, your purpose, and your USP. All of them should start from a central vision and clearly defined goals. Make it clear why they matter to you and how you will go about achieving them. Alignment of your core strategies is paramount and needs to be built intentionally into your business design.

Consider all of the strategies within your brand promise; for example, your communications, pricing, sales and marketing, and growth plans should all connect to your customer strategy. If these don't have common ground to check against, there is a chance that they won't end up supporting the bigger picture, and that is when you get cultural misalignment. This is why I have focused so much on being clear about your brand promise, purpose, and USP. When these have buy-in from everyone, all decisions become easier. And if they don't add value to your end goal or get you there quicker, then why are you doing them? Providing clarity means your employees know whether they are doing the right thing and considering the right initiatives at key decision points, and your external audiences see a consistency that keeps them believing in your brand.

When planning how to design your brand experience, you will need to know where you are heading, what the journey feels like for your audiences, and how to get there. For this, you are going to need a journey map.

The journey map

'Some people do so little thinking, they haven't even got their sail up. You can imagine where they're going to wind up.'

Jim Rohn

Designing your experience journeys intentionally is where strategy moves into design. You may have a process in place to deliver a transaction, but planning the journey is much more than just considering the end result. It needs to consider how your audiences feel along the way – looking not just at processes, but at behaviours and emotions, too.

A journey isn't the same as a touch point. While a touch point may be a transaction, a visit to your website, or a customer in your store at any given moment in time, the journey will consist of many connected parts from various different departments and owners within the company. It may be the 'new business quote journey' or the 'renewal journey'; each one may take place over a period of time, or they may all happen in the same interaction. It all depends on your business model. What is important is that you map out much more than processes: you are looking for the emotional rollercoaster that both the customer and the employee go on in what we call the 'experience curves'.

Experience curves trace the flow of emotions from positive to neutral, or to negative if things are bad, throughout each journey. Your audiences will under- and over-index on emotion at various parts of the journey, and whether that is intentionally planned or not is in your gift.

Craig's Cars - Getting a Quote for Car Insurance

	Awareness	Investigate	Apply	Compare	Decision	Cover
	Understand renewal price & increase	Find out options for new providers	Gain alternative prices and policies	Compare quotes from alt providers	Decide who gives the best option	Put yourself on cover for next yr
	Steve receives renewal notice 14 days before renewal. Not happy that the price has gone up he calls to see why but his existing provider cannot improve it	Steve takes to the internet to look at options whilst he has his morning coffee, to search for alternative options that would suit people like him. Steve uses his tablet to do this	Steve adds a list of suitable links to his clipboard and moves into his office where he sits down to work through the options. He finds out his leisure club has a special scheme for people just like him	Steve gets lots of options from his comparison sites and also directly from Craig's Cars who offer the scheme to his leisure club. They seem to give great cover at a great price	Steve wants to check that the offer is as good as it looks online so he calls Craig's Cars. He gets through to Dave who seems to know what he expects and who offers great service as well	Dave works through the final details with Steve, personalising his policy to give him exactly what he needs whilst staying within budget. His new policy is emailed to him

Channels
- Email renewal
- Renewal invite

- Comparison site
- Call
- Internet

- Comparison site
- Call
- Internet

- Comparison site
- Written quotes

- Online Apply
- Callback

- Customer portal
- Email
- Documents

Thought bubbles:
- "I can't believe this increase"
- "Now I'll need to shop around"
- "There are lots of alternatives"
- "Which one is the best for me?"
- "This is the one I'm going to choose"
- "These guys will look after me"

Trigger
- First time driver
- Replacement car

Persona
Silver Steve
- 45-65
- Trendy mature
- Affluent taste
- Buys quality
- Will pay extra for more value
- Safe driver
- Lives in a nice suburb

Map Key
- Point of Delight
- Point of Pain
- Idea

Pain
- New price going up with no warning or contact
- Knowing Steve is due for his renewal we could send an estimate
- Auto invite personalised from the info we already know
- Opportunity to link all channels

Delight
- The dedicated scheme make Steve feel special
- With a great price & policy matched to Steve as an individual
- And with great service offered tool

Beyond Brand   Love the Experience   Customer Journey Map

While process mapping approaches such as Six Sigma and ISO accreditation are factual, transactional techniques, they don't capture how the customer or the employee feels when going through the journey. In order to do this, you need to capture the range of behaviours and emotions that happen throughout. It is important to map both employee and customer journeys together as one impacts on the other. If you have a part of the journey that is particularly challenging for the employee, for example, navigating through ten different systems at the same time to deliver an outcome, the chances are it will feel arduous to the customer, too. A typical journey will have stress points within it when emotion is high, like registering a home insurance claim, for example, but mostly it should feel easy, secure, trustworthy, and worthwhile. This will make the difference between an experience that is good enough and a memorable one that gets talked about.

If you class the experience as a key part of your marketing budget or retention target, you are likely to think about it differently. It's easy to use the pain points in the journey as benefits for your ROI. Customer experience has real financial benefit in the same way as a new product line or a new service does. Initially prioritise transformation that adds tangible value. A few key wins will make it easier to gain commitment from all stakeholders for the softer intangible benefits in your future initiatives.

Stakeholder engagement plays a key role in getting approval for your budget and resource requirements. Walk stakeholders through the current journeys as if they were the customer. It can sometimes be sobering for an executive leader to say, 'Do we really put our customers through that experience?'

You and your leaders can easily learn to journey map. We teach businesses how to do it for themselves all the time and then to use it as part of their ongoing routine. Whether you use us or try it for yourselves, it is an investment I'm sure will pay off handsomely.

We have included a Customer Journey Mapping Kit for you to use in the downloadable templates, which you can access at www.beyondbrand.org/BBMTemplates

The journey needs to match what your brand promise stands for, mirroring the experience you offer. In order to create a brand experience that is immediately known as yours, you need it to be truly unique. It must feel right.

Let's take a look at whether your brand experience delivers the emotional connection you want to create.

Does it feel right?

'I've learned that people will forget what you said, people will forget what you did, but people will never forget how you made them feel.'

Maya Angelou

A brand experience that feels like it belongs to your business is a difficult thing to articulate, let alone build. The key question to ask is: does it feel right when you walk in your customers' shoes? Use your brand promise as your litmus test.

You don't have to make sure that every single part of the journey feels 'wow'. That would be unrealistic and unsustainable. Instead, look for anything that causes friction or makes the experience difficult for your audiences. Remove elements that cause negative emotions, leaving you with just 'brilliant basics' and 'magic moments'.

Brilliant basics

Brilliant basics are all about getting the basic needs of the customers right every time. Making it easy for your customers to use your services allows them to spend time doing the things they love to do.

Matthew Dixon, author of several fantastic books about the impact of customer experience, has a really simple way of explaining this concept. I interviewed Matthew while writing this book and he explained:

'Unfortunately, many companies think that offering over-the-top service will get customers to buy from them... but the data is very clear that this is a waste of time and money.

This doesn't mean that customer service is unimportant. It's critically important… just not in the way companies tend to think.'

Brilliant basics are important if you want to keep loyal customers. Do the basics consistently well, and customers will know what they are getting from you. If that makes their lives easier and is better than they can get elsewhere, they will continue to use you.

Magic moments

Magic moments, on the other hand, are about delivering the unexpected to surprise and delight your audiences. They make stories and reputations go viral, creating enviable brand loyalty.

STARBUCKS CASE STUDY

Surprise and delight can happen whenever you allow your employees the freedom to do the right thing. Let's take the example of a deaf customer, going into Starbucks to order his Frappuccino. Each day, he would type his order on his phone to show the barista, until one day, his barista used sign language to ask for his order.

She handed him a note explaining, 'I've been learning ASL [American sign language] just so you can have the same experience as everyone else.'

The gesture was priceless. The customer posted the experience to his Facebook account, where it received over 27,000 likes and around 6,000 shares.[28] When your customers share experiences like that, who needs advertising?

Allow your employees the freedom and empowerment to surprise and delight people, within the guidelines you set in your brand promise. I would recommend using standard operating processes (SOPs) while enabling your team to do the right thing, even if it means stepping outside of these guidelines (as long as no legal rules or regulations are affected). Give them the freedom to act quickly and responsibly to make a difference. Allow them to be creative. If they discover a new approach that delivers a better experience, be open to introducing it. Check it fits with your purpose and brand promise, then try it out with some of your best customers. Their feedback will soon tell you if it feels right.

Communicating in the right way with your customers and employees could be the difference between your messages being heard loud and clear, or being misinterpreted and left wanting. How do you ensure your brand promise translates in the way you want it to?

---

28 https://www.facebook.com/MPO.I.Piracha/posts/ten208673727024270

Loud and clear

> *'Positive communication from the service provider is helpful, positive, timely, useful, easy and pleasant; it leaves the customer feeling not only satisfied with the service, but with a positive affect towards the provider.'*

Dr Dwayne Ball

Communicating your brand promise consistently is critical in ensuring that all your audiences are aligned to what makes your brand special and unique. If you don't match the experience with the language, it isn't going to feel right. You need to be genuine, sincere, inspiring, and transparent. Use language that your customers and employees use, and remove any jargon that complicates the message.

Part of knowing your audiences' personalities is about understanding how they expect you to communicate with them. The language that connects you to them needs to shine through all interactions, so that your messages are clear and understood. This is where your tone of voice (TOV) comes into play.

Your TOV is your brand's personality coming out in words. It connects your messages with your audiences' emotions in a consistent manner, displaying your values and your brand promise so that people know what they can expect when they're communicating with you. This breeds familiarity and trust. Without its own distinct TOV, a company runs the risk of its communication being lost. It's not what you say, but how you say it.

The degree of formality you use depends on your brand's personality and how you want to be perceived by your audiences. If you want to be a cool, hip brand like Apple, then your language and marketing will follow that trend, whereas your audiences will probably expect more formality if you are a lawyer or funeral director, unless you're a funeral director who specialises in bespoke cool, hip funerals. Your TOV should largely go unnoticed by your audiences. It is something that should feel natural when they're interacting with your brand.

Involving your audiences in the early stages of creating your TOV can be useful. This helps to ensure your communications hit home, and people will be more likely to be receptive to something they have helped to create. Audience involvement could consist of focus groups, feedback on previous copy, or suggestions for the TOV guidelines. Feedback on your communications is a sure-fire way of establishing whether you have developed a suitable TOV or not. Negative feedback means you may have to rethink things. Think about how you can deliver a consistent feel across different channels and touch points. A letter of apology, for instance, will need to have a different approach to a Twitter message, but both must use your unique TOV.

The most important thing is that a TOV rings true for the people who will connect to it. Look at the approaches you use to connect with your audiences, both internally and externally. People absorb your stories in different ways, so make sure you communicate them without losing their key messages.

Chinese whispers

'The goal is to provide inspiring information that moves people to action.'

Guy Kawasaki

People want to receive information in a way that works best for them, when it suits them. Therefore, your messaging needs to be flexible and varied to suit several preferences.

While nothing beats a face-to-face conversation for personal interaction, it isn't always the most appropriate method of communicating. Technology has progressed at such a pace that with planning and creativity, you can provide options for audiences to download most communications how and when they want them. Recorded video, video conferencing, vlogs, podcasts, Skype, intranet, and blogs can all deliver effective, engaging messaging that frees up time for people.

If you are not on track, the complaints you receive will soon let you know. They are a gift. They are a measure of where things are wrong in your business, so the incentive to resolve them *and* remove the root cause is huge. How many times are complaints resolved without anyone in the business actually working to prevent the same problem happening again? There are many reasons for removing flaws from your business, so I've picked out my top five to give you some food for thought:

- ❖ 82% of consumers say they've stopped doing business with a company due to poor service[12]

- ✿ A 5% increase in customer retention can increase profits by between 25% and 85%[29]

- ✿ 55% of consumers intended to make a purchase, but didn't due to poor service[30]

- ✿ 95% of unhappy customers never complain in a way that means a business can find the complaint[31]

- ✿ 62% of customers report having to contact a business multiple times to resolve an issue[32]

Getting it wrong can be fatal for your business, but getting it right can lead to further loyalty. People are prepared to forgive companies that get things wrong occasionally if they consistently put them right.

Work through the exercise below to identify how you can get the best from your communications and the approach you use to connect with your audiences.

---

29 http://www.bain.com/Images/BB_Prescription_cutting_costs.pdf
30 http://about.americanexpress.com/news/docs/2012x/axp_2012gcsb_us.pdf
31 https://www.1stfinancialtraining.com/Newsletters/trainerstoolkit1Q2009.pdf
32 http://www.convinceandconvert.com/customer-experience/23-statistics-that-show-why-customer-service-mostly-sucks/

EXERCISE 5

Strategy:

* What is your customer strategy?
* Are customers at the heart of all your other strategies?
* Is your customer strategy aligned to your brand promise?

Does it feel right?

* Walk through your customer journeys to see if they feel good
* Go back to the floor for a day to see what reality looks like
* Review your communications approach – is it as good as it could be?
* Do you have a good balance of face-to-face and remote communications?
* Do your internal and external communication approaches complement and match each other?

Perform a TOV review. Do you have a distinct TOV and is it embedded into your business widely and consistently?

Let's get personal

'Personalization wasn't supposed to be a cleverly veiled way to chase prospects around the web, showing them the same spammy ad for the same lame stuff as everyone else sees. No, it is a chance to differentiate at a human scale, to use behavior as the most important clue about what people want and more important, what they need.'

Seth Godin

How can you create individual journeys that are personal to all the customers you have?

Personalisation has evolved with developments in customer data. It can improve sales conversion by up to 14%, as well as increasing the average size of order value, multiplying the benefits to brand value.

Personalisation is difficult to copy, so a customer will view the service as being bespoke and personal. If the experience is one that the customer enjoys, they are likely to feel that other providers will not be able to deliver the same. A tailored service is viewed as more satisfying than a one-size-fits-all delivery, increasing trust and loyalty towards the brand. Engaged customers are 23% more profitable to a brand than those who are not, while actively disengaged consumers cost 13% in lost sales value.

The benefits of customer loyalty have been proven in many studies. The European Customer Satisfaction Index (ECSI) model, created by Ball, Coelho, and Machás (2004), shows the correlation between expectations, perceived quality, and perceived value, which impact satisfaction, and communication, trust, image, and complaints, which drive the strength of loyalty.[33]

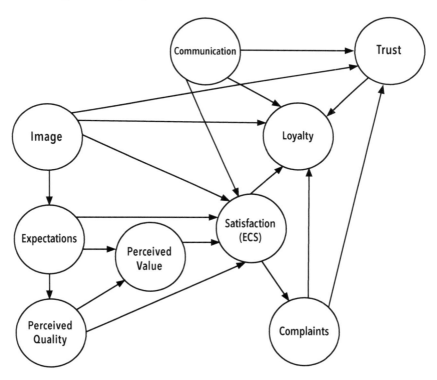

The ECSI model is used across many different industry sectors, such as insurance and financial services. In the model, loyalty involves the following key areas:

33 Reprinted with permission from Emerald Group Publishing Limited, originally published in 'The Employee–Customer Satisfaction Chain in the ECSI Model', *European Journal of Marketing*, Vol. 37, Issue 11/12, pp.1703–1722. © Emerald Group Publishing Limited (2003)

✿ Customer satisfaction – a contributing factor to loyalty, but not the overarching reason for staying with a company

✿ Trust – comes in two formats: credibility trust (belief that the provider will deliver on promises) and benevolence trust (belief that the service provider is acting in the best interests of the customer and will not take advantage of the relationship)

✿ Communication – positive communication is helpful, timely, useful, easy, and pleasant, leaving a customer with a good feeling towards the brand

✿ Image – the more positive the brand image, the greater satisfaction and trust the customer will have in the firm's service, which will impact on loyalty

✿ Complaint handling – badly handled complaints will be interpreted as incompetence, having a negative effect on the brand's credibility and the customers' trust

In 2006, Ball, Coelho, and Vilares added personalisation into the ECSI model, confirming that personalisation has a positive impact on customer satisfaction, trust, and loyalty if it's done in the right way. Personalisation, though, requires flexibility and it has to feel special. You have to be willing to adapt and adjust your offering to suit the needs of your customers. When a product or service feels just that bit different, customers will be prepared to pay handsomely for it.

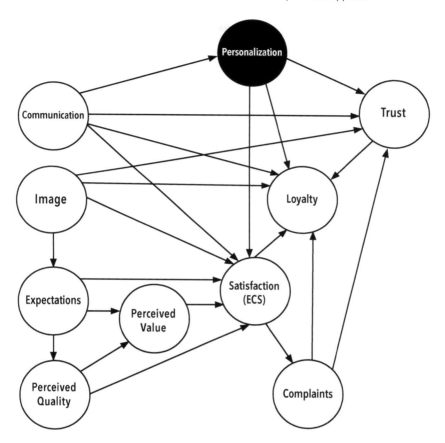

For example, in 2017 Rolls Royce commissioned a one-off project to design a vehicle costing £10 million. It featured a yacht-style Sweptail body, large panoramic roof, and the registration number was shaped within the bodywork. It even included a bespoke mechanical centre console which distributed a bottle of the customer's favourite champagne and two flutes at the press of a button.

In order for personalisation to be seen as good value, communication between the customer and the brand needs to be first class. You have to identify each customer's unique needs and work out how your brand can meet them. When a customer senses that he or she is being personally addressed and cared for, you build what is known as 'customer equity'. The customer believes you know them intimately and they would not get an equal service elsewhere. This generates 'retention equity', which leads to emotional loyalty and a willingness to buy even more services or products from your portfolio.[34] These customers also show indifference to competitors' campaigns, are less affected by price-sensitivity, and give your brand positive word-of-mouth recommendations, delivering maximum individual customer lifetime value and profitability, and fantastic ROI.

They become your biggest brand advocates. Check out these facts about the power of recommendations:

- 87% of customers share good experiences with others
- 69% read positive reviews on social media
- 88% are influenced by online customer service reviews when making buying decisions[35]

Equally, getting it wrong has an impact:

- 95% of customers share bad experiences with others
- 63% of consumers read negative reviews on social media[34]
- 48% of people who had a negative experience told ten or more people about it[36]

---

34 R.T. Rust, V. A. Zeithaml, and K. N. Lemon (2000), *Driving Customer Equity: How Customer Lifetime Value is Reshaping Corporate Strategy*, New York: Free Press.

35 https://www.zendesk.com/resources/customer-service-and-lifetime-customer-value/

36 https://hbr.org/product/harvard-business-review-on-increasing-customer-loyalty/10322-PDF-ENG

Personalisation is your chance to offer a USP which is difficult for your competitors to replicate or replace, and is a differentiator other than price when customers are comparing the market. Use a customer relationship management (CRM) system to help you build processes around knowing your customers and acting on that knowledge. Adding contextualisation to help you shape the experience will make a big difference, so let's look at how you can do that.

You know me so well

'The aim of marketing is to know and understand the customer so well, the product or service fits him and sells itself.'

Peter Drucker

How do you make personalisation work to your advantage? The technology to enable you to do this is now cheap enough to be accessed by businesses of all sizes. By 2020, the digital universe will be 44 trillion gigabytes in size, so in future years the opportunities to know your customers and employees will be even greater. A brand's use of technology to tailor an experience incorporates two opportunities – personalisation and contextualisation.

We've already covered personalisation in depth. If you think about Amazon, you'll see experts in personalisation in action, showing you products you might be interested in based on your buying history.

Contextualisation looks at when customers engage with or purchase from a brand, and why, adding in external factors that may affect them. This could consist of looking at the weather forecast to determine what clothing to show on the home pages, or what offers to show depending on customers' GPS locations. Contextualisation helps brands understand where their customers are on their journey, and uses this insight to personalise the experience across all touch points and channels.

Both personalisation and contextualisation enable you to recommend the most appropriate journeys and offers to your customers, which maximises value for them and profit for your brand. The results speak for themselves: 35% of Amazon's revenue is generated by its recommendation engine,[37] while 75% of Netflix users select movies based on Netflix's recommendations,[38] which leads to them viewing more of what they like and optimising their viewing time. This provides a feeling of value for money, increasing retention of customers.

This type of insight is now available for most brands to apply to their businesses and not just for corporate giants. As you learn more about your customer avatars, you can combine the insights you gain with emotional intelligence and use these trends to influence a better experience. Think about the 'people like me also like' activities that companies such as Amazon and Netflix are using. All they are doing is taking their customer personas, adding in valuable information and analytical learning to make them richer.

This approach has many other benefits:

- ✿ Avoiding offer fatigue, as your offers will be specific, and therefore likely to be seen as valuable

- ✿ Cutting down on wasted marketing activity that doesn't deliver a positive outcome

- ✿ Targeting copycat audiences through Facebook, YouTube, and LinkedIn

- ✿ Adapting your current ways of working to suit customers and improve their journeys

---

37 https://www.mckinsey.com/industries/retail/our-insights/how-retailers-can-keep-up-with-consumers
38 https://medium.com/netflix-techblog/netflix-recommendations-beyond-the-5-stars-part-1-55838468f429

O2 CASE STUDY

O2 investigates trends in conversations, identifying customers' favourite features on different mobile devices and then tailoring assets in a more targeted way.

Daryl West, O2 Telefonica's insight lead, says 'If we can see a spike at the same time each year, we can make sure we have the relevant offers on our Priority app.'[39]

For example, their analysis revealed a peak in conversations about summer holiday plans between February and June, which coincided with a peak in conversations about exercise and fitness training. On the basis of this information, O2 placed offers on its Priority app in February to promote wearable devices to people who were already thinking about getting fit for their getaway to the sun. It's a classic example of how a more personalised customer experience and optimised marketing can lead to an increase in revenue and profit.

---

39 https://www.raconteur.net/business/personalisation-is-key-to-increasing-customer-loyalty

Can you feel it?

> 'Your smile is your logo, your personality is your business card, how you leave others feeling after having an experience with you becomes your trademark.'

Jay Danzie

What makes you different is not always about the physical product, features or benefits of your service. It is actually the experience you are buying and this can make the difference when the same product or service can be bought through a number of different providers. In this scenario advocacy comes predominantly from the experience. The experience is what you feel. You can't see it.

The emotional connection between a person and a brand plays a big part in determining the strength of customer loyalty, so you need a way of measuring it in your insights model. We will look at sentiment analysis further in the Advantage principle, but basically, it is the ability to listen to conversations happening in your business and understand their emotional context. This helps shape your brand experience based on the emotional impact you are delivering to your customers and through your employees. Now that you can listen to the interactions your customers are having in real time across your phone calls, social media, or other digital channels, you will get an accurate view of how they are feeling more quickly than waiting for survey feedback to be processed and analysed through monthly trends.

It is important to understand the emotional experience you want your audiences to have at every stage of interacting with your brand. If your employees are struggling with frustrating system constraints or empowerment barriers, it will stop them delivering a great experience. That will then come out in their interactions, affecting the emotions of customers. Therefore, you need to measure the emotional impact on both employees and customers as they work through the process.

VIRGIN ATLANTIC CASE STUDY

When Virgin Atlantic wanted to transform its business class air travel to be better than anyone else's, it used a version of journey mapping with emotional inclusion to figure out which parts it needed to focus on.[40]

By looking into the stages of the business class trip, Virgin Atlantic was able to see what emotions their customers experienced at each stage and the challenges they faced in trying to make the experience feel like a pleasure rather than a pain. They found that the actual in-flight experience was not the biggest area of emotional impact; customers experienced negative emotions in the stages that preceded and predated boarding the plane. Virgin made it easy by removing negative emotions and filled the gap with positive ones, giving the customers a wow experience.

This is how you stand out and feel different from your competition.

Moments of Truth	Getting to the Airport	Check-in	Comfort until flight	In-flight comfort	Arrival	Getting to destination
Feelings	✿ Stressful ✿ Complicated ✿ Parking ✿ Lugging	✿ Long, frustrating lines ✿ Unnecessary (only necessary to the airline)	✿ Want/need to work ✿ Want/need to relax	✿ Planes are uncomfortable by nature ✿ Long time spent in a seat ✿ Boredom	✿ Unkempt ✿ Unshowered ✿ Clothes a mess	✿ Traffic ✿ Unfamiliar place
Service solution	✿ Transport to airport provided ✿ Driver handles luggage	✿ "Drive-through" check-in ✿ Airline knows where you are	✿ Clubhouse with Internet access, fax, library ✿ Salon, massages, beauty ✿ Sound room, driving range, skiing machine	✿ Full sleeper seats ✿ Mood lighting ✿ Gradual dawn ✿ Bar ✿ You decide meals	✿ Arrival valet ✿ 18 showers ✿ Makeup & shave ✿ Heated floors ✿ Clothes pressed ✿ Hot & cold breakfast	✿ Chauffered delivery to destination ✿ Comfortable ride door-to-door ✿ Knowledge- able local driver

CUSTOMER EXPERIENCE →

Lead the way

> *'You cannot expect your team to rise above your example.'*
>
> **Orrin Woodward**

Leaders are brand ambassadors, bringing the brand promise to life and showing the way for all. They need to inspire everyone around them to achieve the company goals and fulfil its purpose.

If you have selected your leaders carefully then they should have the right personalities to do this naturally. While it is easy to select a leader who is positive, trustworthy, inspirational, and empowering, it is slightly trickier to make sure they are fully behind your purpose.

Purposeful leadership is leading, not managing. A manager gets tasks done, completes to do lists, and ticks boxes. A strong, purposeful leader has followers. They don't even need to be good leaders, although it helps, especially when you're trying to retain good people. Look at the leadership of Elon Musk at Tesla and Space X or Steve Jobs at Apple: people said that they were a nightmare to work for, but their vision and purpose had people follow them in pursuit of the greater good. That quality is what you want in your leadership team. What they must be is clear and focused on the brand promise, the brand experience, and the consistency of the messaging around what it means to be part of the brand. That is what strong purposeful leadership is about.

Communication, leadership, and design all play significant roles in defining your approach and its strategy for delivering brand experience. Evoking the right emotions and personalising your brand to your audience, all the while remaining true to your brand promise, will separate you from the competition.

We'll move into the principle of channels next, but before we do, please complete the exercise below to understand where the strength of your approach is today.

EXERCISE 6

- ❖ What layers of personalisation exist in your business today?

- ❖ What processes could you make more personal?

- ❖ What data and insights are you using to make the journey personal and individual for your best customers?

- ❖ How could you use predictive analytics to assist in bringing flexibility to your decision paths?

- ❖ What could you do to add personalisation to your business and give you competitive advantage?

Principle Four

CHANNELS

Changing channels

> *'Your website isn't the center of your universe. Your Facebook page isn't the center of your universe. Your mobile app isn't the center of your universe. The customer is the center of your universe.'*
>
> **Bruce Ernst**

We may be firmly into a digital world now, but it doesn't mean that traditional communication channels are dead. People still want the experience of going into a store, interacting with people, and touching products. Yes, virtual reality will give customers the flexibility of having these experiences without leaving their lounges, but that isn't going to replace the impact of traditional approaches entirely.

However, e-commerce is definitely having an impact on the way customers shop today. Fewer people are entering stores, instead choosing to shop from the comfort of their own homes, so businesses have to work harder to get people into their stores and keep them engaged. The trick is to include traditional channels with fantastic services, and integrate a seamless experience between those channels and digital enhancements.

UNDER ARMOUR CASE STUDY

Under Armour has 'engagement zones' in its stores, with video walls and interactive games where customers can achieve certain levels and targets, or recreate virtual spaces. In its Chicago store, it has an interactive putting green which allows customers to choose which green they want to play on from famous courses around the world. Customers personalise their products on virtual terminals to make them unique. The flow throughout the store is intentional and makes the customer experience magical and memorable.

Under Armour is building brand fans by integrating digital capabilities and channels into the traditional bricks and mortar store experience.

Customers are looking for helpers, not salespeople. They want someone to show them how to experience the brand's products and capabilities better, to make shopping not only easy and hassle-free, but also an exciting and personal experience. Technology has enhanced our ability to do this, with the only restrictions coming from our imagination, effort, and desire. The internet may have been the start of the digital era, but it has evolved to offer us a very different experience now to when it first was introduced.

Internet evolution

'640K ought to be enough for anybody.'

Bill Gates (1981)

It's hard to remember a world without the internet, but using it in a commercial way is still only around twenty-five years old. Today, many aspects of our physical lives are merging with our online habits – shopping, working, socialising, and watching TV are just a few examples. Since 2010, internet use has grown by 97%, with a 600% rise in mobile use alone.[41]

Previously, the internet was used by businesses to influence consumers. Now people use the internet to decide which businesses they will choose and what actions they will take. That may be a subtle difference, but it is an important one.

The last five years of internet evolution have been huge but we can expect that to continue at pace. Mobile internet has developed and removed restrictions that were there before. The next set of technological advancements will optimise this as artificial intelligence (AI), virtual reality (VR), and automation enter our lives. Lifestyles will change as we are introduced to ways to maximise our time. Automated driving and travel will give us the time to work more effectively. Shopping will incorporate automated ordering, stock replacement, and virtual test drives from the comfort of our homes. As our fridges become filled automatically, we will be picking slots for our dry cleaning to be returned

---

41 http://www.internetworldstats.com/emarketing.htm

to us, by bots in automated cars, at the time when it is convenient for us.

Sounds like something from a sci-fi movie? It's not that far away now. Our expectations will grow as people search out better experiences and seek ways of optimising the one thing that money can't buy: time! Over half of the world's population is now online and owns a smartphone. If your business is to survive in the future, then it will need to take advantage of today's digital world and use it to make people's lives easier.

The digital world

'There is no digital strategy any more, just strategy in a digital world.'

Anon

Digital evolution has created challenges for brands wanting to build meaningful long-term relationships with loyal customers. The power to do so has shifted and now sits clearly with the consumers, as they have access to third-party review sites, online communities, and social media to inform them. They can now research products or brands without ever visiting a store or listening to a marketing message. The digital landscape has changed the expectations required of the brand experience. In order to build a meaningful relationship with customers, brands now have to reach much higher standards, building trust, communicating effectively, and adding the human touch so that the brand delivers a digital experience in line with its brand promise. No wonder CEOs are kept awake at night by the digital transformation.

Digital is here to stay, with new channels and tools, such as instant messaging, chatbots, and virtual assistants, being added all the time. It is part of the customer's toolkit, so you need to integrate it into your brand experience. When you're considering the digital requirements for your brand experience, go back to your brand promise and ensure that it flows through all your digital channels in the same way it flows through the traditional ones. Your customer personas and ideal audiences will drive the extent of the digital expectation of your business, and you need to consider the needs of your next generation of customers, too.

If you are feeling overwhelmed by this migration into digital channels, don't be – 40% of CEOs have digital transformation as their number one priority.[42] The good news is that the technology to deliver an omni-channel experience to your audiences is now advanced and competitively priced. The preferred channel is changing, with the older generations still using the telephone as their first choice, while younger generations tend to prefer social media, only resorting to the telephone as their last choice of communication.

Let's take a look at how the contact centre has changed as digital has entered the equation.

---

42 https://www.globalservices.bt.com/uk/en/news/digital-transformation-top-priority-for-ceos

The contact centre

'The future of communicating with customers rests in engaging with them through every possible channel: phone, email, chat, web, and social networks.'

**Marc Benioff, co-founder and
CEO of Salesforce**

Contact centres have never really been embraced. With an image of offshore sweatshops or onshore outsourcers, they became seen as the new factory environment for workers and a way for large organisations to take the cost out of serving customers. Despite these perceptions, the contact centre has remained consistent in delivering customer care, sales, and services for many organisations. Most medium or large organisations have some form of centralised telephone channel, either in-house or outsourced. The best ones deliver a solid, dependable performance that is consistent with the brand promise. The expected customer experience standard is now to be omni-channel connected.

A channel strategy is about knowing the channel preferences of your audiences and building them into a connected experience. This goes back to understanding your audiences, knowing what they expect from your brand, and delivering a consistently high-class experience whenever they need to get in touch with you.

Research shows that 67% of customers would rather self-serve than speak to someone,[43] and 84% of customers have

---

43   https://whatsnext.nuance.com/customer-experience/giving-customers-independence-digital-self-service/

used businesses' self-serve, FAQs, or online apps in the last twelve months.[44] With the introduction of AI and technology like Alexa delivering solutions for menial tasks, this is definitely a trend that is only going to get stronger. In fact, Gartner predicts that by 2020, customers will manage 85% of their relationships with an enterprise without interacting with a human.[45]

Only 26% of companies offer self-service tools for consumers via their mobile applications at present, so there is some way to go.[46] However, with the speed of technology advancements and the rate of adoption through the digital generations, it won't be long before this type of customer experience will become mainstream. The contact centre will evolve to assist self-service channels and digital options. But if the experience is emotive, painful, or sensitive, make sure you have human contact options easily available, as that is still the default choice when things get tricky. Jobs in contact centres in the future will require a certain level of emotional intelligence, social skills, and an ability to communicate on multiple platforms, including third-party sites and social media channels, to deliver consistent levels of customer engagement.

44 https://www.forrester.com/Nearly+70+Of+Consumers+Complain+Online+
    About+Poor+Customer+Service/-/E-PRE8844
45 https://www.gartner.com/imagesrv/summits/docs/na/customer-360/
    C360_2011_brochure_FINAL.pdf
46 http://www.bradcleveland.com/resources/statistics/

To get social, you have to be social

'A brand is no longer what we tell the consumer it is – it is what consumers tell each other it is.'

Scott Cook, co-founder, Intuit

Social media exploded into our lives at the start of the new millennium as the internet started to build digital communities. The world has come a long way since the introduction of Facebook in 2004. Facebook grew quickly in popularity, outpacing MySpace, LinkedIn, and Friends Reunited, and by 2009 it was the most used social network on the planet.

In 2005, YouTube brought video into our lives. The first video to reach 1 million views was a Nike advertisement featuring Ronaldinho in September 2005, and by December of that year the site was getting 8 million views a day. By July 2006, YouTube users were uploading 65,000 videos a day and it was getting 100 million views a day. Today, estimates indicate that more than 300 hours of video are uploaded to YouTube every minute.

The year 2007 saw the introduction of a device that would change the way we communicate for ever: the iPhone. Steve Jobs's legendary speech at MacWorld 2007 saw the release of three revolutionary products:

* A widescreen iPod with touch controls
* A revolutionary phone
* A breakthrough internet device

The smartphone was easy to use and provided mobile access to many features we could previously only access from our desktop computers. The app changed the way we would use media forever. Heavily influential in the spread of social media, the smartphone would become the new best friend of the teenager, revolutionise the way we use a phone, and start the growth of mobile internet use. By 2009, businesses were starting to experience the impact social media could have on a brand's reputation and commercial value if they got things wrong.

While travelling with his band, Dave Carroll witnessed from the window of his plane how badly the airline handled his band's instruments. His precious Taylor guitar was destroyed as baggage handlers threw it around with the other luggage being loaded onto the baggage cart. He recorded a video of the event, launching it on YouTube on 6 July 2009. Within twenty-four hours it had had 150,000 hits, and within four days it had had over 500,000 views. Within four weeks it had wiped $180 million off the share price of the airline! If you haven't seen the video, then check out the link below to see the full effect.[47]

The way in which we interact with brands has changed – 56% of consumers are active on more than one social network,[48] while over a quarter of all adults participate in the various formats of the sharing economy,[49] from rooms, cars, and bikes to internet sharing and person-to-person

---

47 https://youtu.be/5YGc4zOqozo
48 http://www.pewinternet.org/2016/11/11/social-media-update-2016/
49 https://www.ons.gov.uk/economy/economicoutputandproductivity/
    output/articles/thefeasibilityofmeasuringthesharingeconomy/
    november2017progressupdate

loans. People connect with a brand through stories rather than through traditional advertising approaches. Stories trigger emotions, and consumers associate those emotions with the brand. They build the connection through content marketing, which starts to build the loyalty.

Marketers now invest in this approach more than in traditional approaches. In 2016, 76% of B2B marketers produced more content than they had done in 2015,[50] and it is proving to be commercially successful. Companies with an active blog generate 67% more leads than those without one,[51] and videos are also becoming more widespread. The shoe retailer Schuh reported four times the conversion rate and a 10% increase in average order value for sessions involving video instead of text chat.[52] By 2019, 80% of internet traffic will be video.[53] If you are not currently investing in video content for your business, now is the time to change that.

Check out some of the recent social facts from industry experts:

- ✿ The most popular content marketing tactic reported by 90% of B2C businesses is social media[54]

- ✿ Social media marketing budgets are projected to double over the next five years[55]

---

50 http://contentmarketinginstitute.com/wp-content/uploads/2015/09/2016_B2B_Report_Final.pdf

51 http://socialmediab2b.com/2012/03/b2b-social-media-leads-infographic/

52 http://blog.3clogic.com/is-video-based-customer-service-the-next-big-thing

53 https://www.cisco.com/c/en/us/solutions/collateral/service-provider/visual-networking-index-vni/complete-white-paper-c11-481360.html

54 http://contentmarketinginstitute.com/2015/10/b2c-content-marketing-research/

55 https://www.socialfresh.com/marketing-statistics-every-cmo-should-know-in-2014/?utm_medium=Webbiquity.com

- 66% of marketers believe social media marketing is core to their business[56]

- In 2015, the average brand generated 87.5 social media posts per channel per month[57]

- 93% of organisations use social media as their main content marketing tactic[38]

Do you need your content to be on all platforms? No, but you do need to understand which platforms and media your ideal customers are using and make sure you dominate on those platforms in your market. We'll discuss the technology and devices that can help you to optimise this opportunity in the next section. Before that, please take a look at the exercise below and review how your business can improve its channel strategy to deliver a better brand experience.

---

56 https://www.salesforce.com/blog/2015/01/2015-state-of-marketing.html
57 https://trackmaven.com/blog/content-marketing-strategy-report/

EXERCISE 7

* Channels audit – what channels do you use today? Are they the ones your MVCs use? What are the gaps for improvement/areas? Look at the ROI and business case for these improvements. Consider a one-to-one with a technical expert to run through the requirements.

* How integrated are your channels? Are you omni-channel ready?

I've seen the future

*'Any sufficiently advanced technology is
indistinguishable from magic.'*

Arthur C. Clarke

Customers are more technology savvy than most businesses now, and larger businesses are struggling to adopt technology quickly enough. Aside from the leading technology players such as Google, Apple, and Amazon, few businesses are able to break new ground in terms of the experience they're offering to customers. At best, they are struggling to keep up and adopt new methods into their business operating models to remain competitive.

If you are a smaller business, you are more agile in meeting customers' changing requirements, and the ease of technology adoption means that these are changing much more frequently. The introduction of cloud technology means you can have access to licences, pay for them on a monthly basis, and have maintenance included as part of the service – a far cry from when you had to purchase physical equipment and require installation support.

Customers will expect you to be careful with their data and security; it is part of the trust they place in your brand. Businesses of all sizes are vulnerable to cyberattack, as much from teenage hackers as sophisticated criminals. You require increased protection from cybercrime, but solutions exist for businesses of all sizes and shapes. You only have to look at recent examples of hacked brands to see the commercial impact it can have on a company's reputation. When teenage hackers attacked one of the big telecommunications providers, it compromised the data of over 150,000 customers, resulting in its share price dropping by a third, and over 100,000 customers left the brand.

Technology opens up opportunities to differentiate your audiences' experience. With advanced analytics that allow you to understand your customers fully, you can design journeys that feel like they have been tailored for each customer.

Let's imagine a scenario that may occur today.

A customer is looking at a product online from one of the brands they like to use. The online device recognises the customer and logs them into their account for convenience. This automatically allows the digital solution to know their shopping habits from previous purchases. It is learning all the time by listening and watching the pages the customer visits and the time it takes them to move between activities. The CRM has recognised what persona the customer falls into, which allows it to shortlist a number of products that may be of interest to the customer on each page they visit.

After they've been on a page for a while and selected multiple similar products, the automated chatbot contacts the customer to see if they need any help. The chatbot reads the text the customer inputs and analyses their sentiment, as well as looking at the product listing that would best suit them. It pushes forward the most appropriate products on the basis of the conversation, which saves the customer time and opens up the discussion to any further questions they may have. By looking at their previous purchases, the chatbot can recommend the best spec and colour combination to make the customer's purchase look great. At the same time, it offers any add-ons that complement and protect the product with a tailored personalisation. It adds all the details into the CRM and offers delivery at a time when the customer is usually at home. We are not looking into the future here; this technology and journey exists today.

With the integration of systems and advanced machine learning, analytics can optimise the customer journey and remove the pain from purchases, making customers feel exclusive and personalising their journey while reducing the need for human interaction (unless the customer wants it). The opportunity exists for you to wow your customers today. The rise of the machines is coming, and it brings with it lots of amazing opportunities.

The rise of the machines

'Only those who attempt the absurd will achieve the impossible.'

M. C. Escher

AI is improving all the time and being woven into our lives through a spectrum of intelligent implements. Robots are replacing humans in manufacturing and autonomous vehicles are removing the need to drive, all with the intention of making us more productive or freeing up time for us to do the things we enjoy.

If a brand can give its customers some of their precious time back, then it will be seen as delivering value. Time is difficult to put a price on. Oracle estimates that over 80% of brands will be using chatbots as part of their customer experience by 2020, while more than one in three brands say customers and prospects prefer to complete a purchase or resolve issues without speaking to a human, if possible.[58]

Our current use of conversation-based interfaces is focused around microphone-enabled devices, for example, speakers, smartphones, virtual PAs (VPAs), or the use of chatbots for the companies that were early adopters of such devices. However, we will start to see this type of interaction adopted by more businesses, governments, and communities as it grows in popularity, with a range of connected devices to form a fluid experience and lifestyle. VPAs perform functions such as prioritising tasks, prompting people to remember important

---

58 https://www.oracle.com/uk/corporate/pressrelease/oracle-report-can-virtual-experiences-replace-reality-vr-chatbots-for-cx-20161206.html

things, or highlighting articles and content they may find interesting. AI is also being used commercially, for example, virtual customer assistants are designed to help customers self-serve or with customer service queries.

Immersive technologies such as virtual reality (VR) and augmented reality (AR) will transform the way individuals interact with brands in the future. VR has now become mainstream, with affordable releases from Samsung and PlayStation, and it won't be long before this technology makes its way into more customer experiences. By 2020, 78% of brands expect to be using VR for customer experiences, with 34% already having implemented the technology to some degree.[59]

AR is already being trialled significantly. When this technology is integrated into mobile phones, customers will be guided on their shopping trips to see items that are recommended for purchasing. VR and AR capabilities will merge with existing digital and traditional channels, seamlessly orchestrating a personalised flow of information through relevant apps and services on our various devices. Integration with multiple mobile, wearable, and smart devices will be enabled by the internet of things (IoT), creating immersive experiences and enabling people to interact with the brands they love in rich environments. Rooms, spaces, and products will come alive through a virtual connection, and customers will test them in virtual worlds before deciding whether to purchase the real thing. Such an experience could see us test driving a new car

---

59 https://www.oracle.com/uk/corporate/pressrelease/oracle-report-can-virtual-experiences-replace-reality-vr-chatbots-for-cx-20161206.html

without even leaving our home, or positioning a sofa in our lounge while we're still in the department store, or wearing clothes virtually and viewing them in our mirrors at home before even placing an order online. The world of shopping as we know it is about to change drastically.

IoT is gaining momentum, supplying physical objects that go beyond traditional programming, and exploiting AI and machine learning to display advanced behaviours and interact more naturally with surroundings and people. Gartner expects us to see an increase in this area, with a shift from stand-alone intelligent devices and equipment to a more collaborative model where they work together.

Over 6.4 billion connected things were in place in 2016, according to Gartner, up 30% on 2015 figures.[60] Smart devices are becoming more mainstream and connected with each other, especially in home and lifestyle products. Watches and TVs have been joined by products like Amazon's Echo, giving us virtual PAs in our homes to make our lives easier.

Companies are introducing the use of digital twins within their operating models. A digital twin recreates a physical product or system as a digital equivalent and uses dynamic software to improve it remotely. Using different types of data, a digital twin can look at the current state of a product and decide what changes need to be made to optimise its performance without even being in the presence of the physical object. Within the next few years, organisations will mirror products and solutions in virtual worlds, enabling them to predict equipment failure, fix things even before

---

60 https://www.gartner.com/newsroom/id/3165317

they break, and plan servicing at the optimum time. Companies will then become more proactive, offering experiences that show how much they care about their customers. Those who adopt this type of approach first will win lots of advocates.

The way in which you use technology from all these advancements to connect with your audiences will affect the strength of your brand experience. What connects your audiences to these experiences will be the devices and interfaces they use.

These are becoming more and more intertwined in the digital and physical experiences, meaning how we design these experiences requires much more thought than looking at the devices in isolation. Let's take a look at how devices can work together to deliver experiences we could have only dreamed of a few years ago.

More smart than a phone

'If your plans don't include mobile, your plans are not finished.'

Wendy Clarke, Coca-Cola

People are always connected these days – 55% of owners reach for their smartphone within fifteen minutes of waking up.[61] The use of apps in people's lives, from both a personal and business perspective, is the new norm. We are always on. It's just the world we live in now, always connected, minds constantly whirring.

Devices have become all-encompassing, consuming people's time so they are constantly looking for ways to grab more time back again. Innovators are constantly looking for 'smart time', where we can use the development of smart devices to give ourselves some time back. Smartphones enable people to use their downtime to continue to be productive by being online more. Previously things such as travel were accepted as time killers; now, wherever you are, you almost certainly expect to have Wi-Fi and connectivity. When automated vehicles are introduced people will use the time they would have spent driving to do the things they need to do, making the most of the 'dead time' effectively, whether that be for work or personal tasks. The average commute can be over two hours a day, so commuters want to use that time meaningfully – 86% said

---

61 https://www.deloitte.co.uk/mobileuk/

they would use personalised commuting services if they were available.[62]

Brands have to be highly mobile to be successful today. Mobile commerce is expected to triple in usage over the next few years, and the generations who are comfortable with this approach are going to play a big part in this. Smartphones play a crucial role when customers come to purchase products and services: 93% of people who use mobile to research go on to make a purchase,[63] 51% of sales now come from mobile devices, and that trend will rise, as it is greater in the digital generations.[64] Customers may start their research on their smartphone and then transfer to their laptop or desktop to complete the purchase, or reserve a product on mobile and complete the transaction in-store. The multi-device approach is all part of time saving. If you want to compete then you simply have to have a mobile strategy.

Amazon has one of the best results in this area as the checkout process is simple. Over 28% of consumers have started to pay for something with other companies and then abandoned the purchase because the checkout process was too complex.[65] It should be as easy to purchase online as it is to reserve something in-store. Make this process simple, easy and secure, and you will steal a march on your competitors.

---

62   https://www.ericsson.com/thinkingahead/the-networked-society-blog/2016/02/08/smart-commuter-10-hot-consumer-trends/

63   https://www.thinkwithgoogle.com/_qs/documents/711/mobile-path-to-purchase-5-key-findings_research-studies.pdf

64   https://www.imrg.org/media-and-comment/press-releases/over-half-of-online-sales-now-made-through-mobile-devices/

65   https://baymard.com/lists/cart-abandonment-rate

There are other devices entering our lives and these trends are affecting consumer behaviour. Let's consider a few recent additions and look at what's coming in the next few years.

Let's get involved

'The internet will disappear. There will be so many IP addresses, so many devices, sensors, things that you are wearing, things that you are inter-acting with, that you won't even sense it.'

Eric Schmidt, Google

Brand interaction is a key part of the in-store experience now. Video screens, sport simulators, fashion shows, celebrity cooking demonstrations, or virtual shooting ranges have become part of the enjoyment. John Lewis recently introduced a brand experience desk where customers choose anything from male personal shoppers to brow and nail bars. This differentiator sets the company apart from high street competitors while playing directly into John Lewis's brand promise.

Wearable technology has boomed in the health and fitness industry, meaning that people are becoming less reliant on smartphones. One in every two consumers believes that smartphones will be a thing of the past within five years as AI progression removes the need for screen inter-action.[50]

One of the next areas of technological progression will be internables – sensors and microchips that are inserted under the skin to measure our wellbeing. Eight out of ten consumers would like to use technology to enhance sensory perceptions and cognitive abilities such as vision, memory, and hearing.[50] The future as we see it in sci-fi movies could be closer than you think.

Clearly the world as we know it today will evolve dramatically if all that is predicted to arrive by 2020 turns into reality. As new devices are introduced, the integration of these devices will get much more complicated. Keep it as simple as possible by ensuring that every device you use communicates with others at every touch point.

It's good to talk

'The computer is incredibly fast, accurate, and stupid. Man is unbelievably slow, inaccurate, and brilliant. The marriage of the two is a force beyond calculation.'

Leo Cherne

Being specific about whom you want to attract means that you can select what proposition you need to offer them and what channels you will use. However, having all the channels and devices working together smoothly is crucial to serving your audiences better than anyone else. Equally, your employees need the right tools to do the job if they are to serve the customers in the best way they can. If all the information you collect is on different databases, then both the customer and employee journey will be challenging.

When you're looking at the journey for your audiences, the devices they're using to touch your brand need to be part of the equation. If 90% of your audiences are moving between devices as part of the journey,[66] then you'd better make sure this is easy to do or you'll lose customers and employees.

Take Apple, for example. I can start something on my iPhone, and then move between my Mac and MacBook as I travel without worrying whether all of my files are syncing. Dropbox and Evernote connect with all my Apple devices, so I have confidence everything will just work. All brands need to aspire

---

66 https://www.thinkwithgoogle.com/insights/library/studies/the-new-multi-screen-world-study/

to create that same feeling of confidence, that simple experience, that single version of the truth.

Here are some tips to keep it simple:

- Pick solutions and vendors that are proven at delivering what you need and can show you examples of it in action

- Devise your technology roadmap for the next five years as a minimum

- Break the cycle of considering equipment and solutions implemented in your business in isolation

- Have as few systems as possible in the infrastructure, to reduce integration dependencies; knowing what each of the systems can and can't do helps you to make informed decisions

- Make sure all the data sources connect into a centrally controlled data warehouse: insights are more powerful when they're pooled together

Of course, some things will change as new tech is introduced, but if you follow these simple rules, you won't go far wrong.

It's important to have a single view of the customer, where all customer interactions and history are captured in one place. With open interfaces and application programming interfaces (APIs) making it simple to link systems together, there is no excuse for not making this happen in your business. Companies that know what their audiences' expectations are can move quickly and cheaply into a fully integrated model and provide class-leading customer experiences. Smaller or medium-sized businesses can do this more quickly than large corporates, who struggle with the size and scale of legacy solutions. Corporates that want to continue to lead their markets need to start behaving like entrepreneurial start-ups, which are nimble, agile and able to change track quickly.

Focus on the devices that matter to your target audiences, optimising those areas and making sure you are delivering an amazing brand experience where your audiences choose to be.

One experience

> *'The more you are like yourself, the less you are like anyone else, which makes you unique.'*

Walt Disney

Once you have outlined what is different about your brand, you then need to ensure that brand consistency is delivered seamlessly across all channels and touch points. By knowing your customers' expectations, you will be able to design the right journeys to deliver against those expectations.

Brand consistency should apply through both the purchase and ownership experiences. Your brand needs to deliver the same promise throughout each stage of the ownership cycle if it is to gain trust, credibility, and lifetime value, all while adding strong commercial value.

The Coca-Cola brand is worth 50% of the company's total value. In hard currency, that's $73 billion. Because Coca-Cola communicates a consistent brand message in all its channels and touch points globally, it can charge a 112% premium for its brand.[67]

The foundation for delivering your brand consistently lies in educating your employees on what it stands for. Your employees must have the tools to be able to bring this to life in their roles, with easy access to all the ingredients you have pulled together. They need to understand these ingredients and believe in them to ensure the message

---

67 http://www.thedrum.com/opinion/2015/08/19/how-achieve-ultimate-asset-brand-consistency

can be passed on effectively to the customer. Use examples and stories of the brand promise in your marketing, share them in the right places, and you will quickly become known for those elements.

Once you do that consistently, you will feel dependable to your audiences. Your brand personality will shine through and be instantly recognisable. If your social media voice is silly and playful, but your product packaging is plain and boring, you'll be sending mixed messages that will confuse your customer and leave them feeling as if your brand can't be trusted.

Customers like predictability. It removes the guesswork and allows them to trust your brand. They then instantly recognise an advert or a piece of marketing with your look and feel, message and values. They know what they are getting.

The one thing you can't buy

'Nothing is as fast as the speed of trust.'

Stephen Covey

Time is the most valuable commodity we have. People expect faster outputs and instant availability. Competing with this is a generation that values time spent doing the things they love over being married to the job. If you are in business now, living up to these expectations can be difficult.

The speed of service through improved technology can assist you in this. People now use social media as a sign-in method to access digital services, showing the amount of trust they have in social brands to allow them to authenticate for us. We want the easy option. We are now using voice biometrics more frequently, and fingerprint or retina recognition will become more natural, both of which deliver a quicker experience. The identity of things (IDoT) will be crucial to manage identity access in a secure way. These identities will then be used to define relationships between devices, humans, applications, services – the list goes on.

As 90% of consumers now expect businesses to have a 24/7 self-service channel,[68] developing this option will be crucial for future customer satisfaction. Today's younger generations have no concept of waiting for something. The thought of being available to watch a TV programme at the same time each week is totally alien to them. Same-day

---

68 Microsoft Global State of Multichannel Customer Service Report

deliveries are expected now, with Amazon already testing delivery by drone within thirty minutes.

People will continue to want to get time back in their lives. If they cannot eradicate dead time, then personalising it to make it relevant and productive will be the next best step. They will be looking for areas that can manage workflow, whether that is in their business or personal lives. They will expect work to go to the appropriate people automatically at the most effective times, creating virtual queues and integrating with other systems and processes.

IDoT will play a huge part in how we achieve these savings. IDoT will enable all devices, applications, and people to work together, while achieving the required security in the digital world. All of this will become standard in what you offer, which is the next principle in our methodology.

Before we move on to that, please take the time to answer the questions in Exercise 8.

EXERCISE 8

- How can your business harness the power of new channels?

- How are you able to save your customers time by optimising self-service and digital channels?

- How mobile ready is your business?

- Where are the potential handoff points in your journeys that require you to consider device and channel switching? Are customers able to do this seamlessly?

- Have you created a single view of the customer?

Principle Five

OFFER

What have you got to offer?

'Your premium brand had better be delivering something special, or it's not going to get the business.'

Warren Buffett

Do your products or services give you a competitive advantage? Are they a superior proposition to your competitors', or are they roughly the same? What stops your competitors taking any edge you have?

On average, it now takes between six weeks and six months to copy a product,[69] but it can take three to five years to change the culture of a business.[70] To ensure that you offer a great proposition for your audiences, having an enviable culture and approach will be much harder to copy.

When McCarthy first formed the marketing mix into a model in 1960, there were four elements – product, price, place, and promotion, with a further three – process, people, and physical evidence – added by Booms and Bitner in 1981. Recently an eighth was added – productivity or performance, depending on who is using the model.[71]

The **product** should always fit the solution consumers want it for. It should represent good value for money (**price**). PR, advertising, sales promotion, etc, are used to **promote** the

69 B.I. Newman (1999), *The Mass Marketing of Politics: Democracy in an Age of Manufactured Images,* Thousand Oaks, CA: Sage Publications, Inc.
70 http://www.modernsurvey.com/blog/20-years-for-cultural-change
71 https://www.professionalacademy.com/blogs-and-advice/marketing-theories---the-marketing-mix---from-4-p-s-to-7-p-s

message to the correct audiences in the manner they would most like to hear it. The product should be available in the **place** the target consumers find it easiest to purchase from.

From front-line sales staff to the CEO, having the right **people** is essential to your business offering. The consistency and effectiveness of your service delivery can vary considerably depending on your business, but it is critical to have **processes** that match the customers' expectations. The **physical evidence** of the product should live up to expectations, whether it is a digital product customers receive through digital communication, PDF documentation, or portal access, or a physical product that is purchased in a store.

Customers want a **quality** product that performs well, and to experience **productivity** improvements as a result of their purchase.

All of these elements are critical for success. If you can deliver them consistently, you will have a head start on your competition. Remember the 'me too' brands? They predominantly offer the same as their competition. Brands that fall into this category can end up winning business because their competitors do not fulfil one of the eight elements effectively. If what you sell can be bought elsewhere, then you need to offer something more to command a premium for your products or services.

But not all brands are affected by this, so what is it that they are doing differently? Some can even ask for a premium over what their competitors charge for a similar proposition.

Apple is a good example of this. This company has built consumer trust because of the consistency of the brand experience it offers. It delivers quality products and has created a differentiated brand promise, which makes Apple an easy choice for their audiences.

If you are to disrupt the market, you need to offer something different, unique, and personalised to cause customers to move from the easy choice, otherwise you will end up being another 'me too' proposition. One way to do this is to keep attracting the best people to work for your brand, and you'll only do that by improving your employee offer.

What's in it for me?

'The competition to hire the best will increase in the years ahead. Companies that give extra flexibility to their employees will have the edge in this area.'

Bill Gates

Do you value the employee experience as much as you do the customer experience? Your people deliver the brand experience to your customers and prospects every single day, so if they are not brand advocates, you won't have much hope of creating a brand that is loved by your target audiences.

As far back as 1994, when James L. Heskett, W. Earl Sasser, and Leonard Schlesinger introduced the Service Profit Chain, it was clear how it would contribute to making a brand successful. The chain is:

- Create a great place to work
- Hire great people
- Pay and treat them well
- Ensure they have the tools to do their jobs well

This leads to highly engaged employees and improves productivity and retention. Happy employees treat customers to amazing service, which creates happy customers, leading to profitable revenue growth and success for the brand. Put the employee first and they will look after the customers, which will look after the profitability of the company.

The hard part is knowing what constitutes a great place to work. What does a great reward package look like? What tools do you need to enable employees to do a great job? A survey by Glassdoor showed 57% of participants would rather have extra benefits over a pay rise.[11] The benefits they chose when looking for a new employer were as follows:

* Healthcare insurance (eg, medical, dental): 40%

* Paid time off: 37%

* Performance bonus: 35%

* Paid sick days: 32%

* Retirement plan and/or pension plans: 31%

The right benefits and salary packages mattered most to employees who were looking for a new employer, but when they were asked what kept them with their current employer, the list was very different. [72]

* Culture and values (26%)

* Career opportunities (21%)

* Senior leadership (16%)

* Work–life balance (13%)

* Compensation and benefits (12.5%)

* Business outlook (12%)

If you're looking to attract the best talent, you need to offer more than just money. But if you are to keep great people in your business you need to offer a great culture. The best people want to work for the best companies.

---

72 https://www.glassdoor.com/research/does-money-buy-happiness-the-link-between-salary-and-employee-satisfaction/

Of course, the factors that attract the best employees will vary according to industry and generation demographics, but the above lists provide some information on how to attract and retain talent today. They show the value that the purpose and the brand promise have in recruiting and keeping the right people. It isn't just about what you offer, though; it's about the way that you offer it.

It ain't what you do, it's the way that you do it

'If you don't have a competitive advantage, don't compete.'

Jack Welch

What you offer your target customers is important in terms of fulfilling their needs, but delivering the same offer differently could make all the difference. Look at Uber, for example. The Uber app has taken away all the problems of ordering a taxi, disrupting an industry that had been stagnant for years.

If you are introducing a difference into an industry that has existed for some time, it could transform people's lives, especially if it makes things easier. Tesla entered the automotive industry with the goal to 'accelerate the advent of sustainable transport by bringing compelling mass market electric cars to market as soon as possible'. Difficult to achieve? Definitely. Difficult to copy? I'd say so. But it wasn't as if they'd entered a market that didn't exist already.

Cars have been widely available since Henry Ford created the Model T in 1908, and the lithium-ion battery has been used commercially since 1991, when Sony released a product using it. What Tesla has done is to combine the two industries and use their respective technologies together to create a new product – one that is differentiated in the market and that people will pay handsomely for.

When you are changing the options for a customer, you either want to make things easier for them and give them some time back, or you want to provide a personal experience that makes them feels special. Delivering satisfaction with the least amount of friction will always win brand fans and gain you a reputation, especially if you do it differently from the rest of the market.

Intelligent personalisation makes it possible for companies to learn and understand what a customer's wants and needs are before personalising their offers to match or surpass those expectations. Using management information, you can create a personalised journey by audience or customer type, picking the elements that deliver a positive emotion for each customer. You don't even have to offer huge proposition differentiation; you can simply offer your best customers whatever makes them feel special or connects them to the person in your company that they like to deal with most.

By identifying who your best customers are, you can then look to differentiate the offer you put in front of them. This is really powerful in terms of personalisation as the customer experiences a service that feels as if it has been tailored for them. Being the same but different just requires a little effort. Think differently, and all of a sudden your proposition no longer looks expensive, but good value.

Not expensive, good value

> 'Design is not just what it looks like and feels like. Design is how it works.'
>
> **Steve Jobs**

When does something stop being expensive and instead represent good value? When it is worth the price to the person paying for it. In fact, 86% of customers are willing to pay up to 25% more for a great customer experience,[21] so why are many businesses still obsessed with price being a barrier to selling products and services?

Price is the fundamental cost consumers pay a business for something when they haven't got any emotional attachment to it. It doesn't mean the product isn't worth more; it just means that the business hasn't explained its worth to the right audiences in a way that resonates with them. People buy emotionally and justify the purchase rationally, so unless you connect your brand to an emotion, customers will need a rational reason to buy it.

Singapore has one of the highest ratios of Ferrari sales per person in the world, yet owning a Ferrari there makes no sense whatsoever. A Ferrari costs about four times more in Singapore than it does in the UK, and the country's top speed limit is 90kph, so why do so many people own one? They don't buy a Ferrari because they need one; they buy it because they want one.

Align your proposition with the value it will bring to your ideal audiences, and explain why it will bring this value. If you have several personas in your audiences, you need to have an offer that is ideal for each of them. Split your customer mix into good, better, and best categories according to how well they fit your brand, then see how well your offer fits their wants and needs. Once you can match the value of your offer with the individual customer types, you can deliver an experience which ticks all their boxes and connects with their emotions.

Saving time is a key factor which will switch the decision-making process from a rational one to an emotive one, but there are others:

Easy process to complete and understand. Make the process easy for customers and they will be grateful. Then they will associate the emotion of gratitude with your brand.

Mobile ease. Customers want flexibility to complete interactions. See how you can intertwine the mobile experience with getting things done.

Feel-good factor. If your brand is connected to making people feel good then their opinions of you will be high.

Personalisation. When you are on the same level as your audiences, they know that all your communications are relevant to them and that you respect their time.

Feel the quality. If you can prove the long-lasting quality of your offer, along with the fact that it feels nice to own, then you are on to a winner. Most people will take a long-term view when they're looking at an investment, providing it will give them value for money and be more enjoyable along the way.

Relationship, not transaction. A big part of brand trust comes from customers having a relationship with the brand, rather than just transacting with it. When customers know they can rely on you, they feel confident in your brand.

Listening to and actioning feedback. Listening builds trust, which is crucial to a long-term relationship. Have a two-way relationship with your audiences rather than selling to them.

Reliability and consistency. If your customers know they will get a consistent and reliable offer when they choose your brand, they won't have to worry about the quality they will receive.

Rarity. It makes a person feel special if they have something rare or limited. Having that emotion linked to your brand is gold dust.

Surprise and delight with 'magic moments'. Go the extra mile to deliver an amazing experience.

There are many areas that deliver you an ROI. I pulled together a paper covering the main ones, and you can find a copy of it at http://www.beyondbrand.co/the-roi-of-customer-experience/.

In the next chapter, we will move on to the sixth principle, exploring how you can make sense of all the data to give you an advantage. Before we do that, please complete the exercise below to consider how strong your current offer is.

EXERCISE 9

Customer:

⚙ What is the USP of your offer? What makes you different?

⚙ How does it feel different?

⚙ List the competitors that offer what you do and compare the unique points of your offer

⚙ Could an independent person explain the value of your offer?

⚙ What would make your audience pay 25% more for it?

Employee:

⚙ How does your employee proposition compare to the market?

⚙ Does your working environment make employees feel valued?

⚙ What degree of flexibility do you have in your current employee proposition?

⚙ How would you describe your culture today?

⚙ How would your employees describe it?

⚙ What would make you the employer of choice in your industry?

Principle Six

ADVANTAGE

What do you know?

'The world is now awash in data and we can see consumers in a lot clearer ways.'

Max Levchin, PayPal

Big Data. We now have more data than we could have ever imagined. But what difference does it make? Unless you know what to do with it then it means very little. Those who do use it well, though, are able to make better decisions and deliver an experience that feels very personalised. In order to be successful, you need the ability to capture and control data while complying with relevant regulations like the Data Protection Act and the General Data Protection Regulation. Those who do not comply face big fines, so make sure you don't fall into that trap.

Data is available from more different sources than ever before:

* Transactional data
* Customer surveys
* Sentiment/emotional analysis
* Customer feedback
* Complaints

Which information should you be using and which don't you need to keep? The answer will be different for each business, so it is important that you set principles for establishing a strong data structure. Prioritise quality over quantity, having a clear view as to what data will enable you to make better decisions, provide value for your audiences, and create a better brand experience.

In *Thinking with Data*, Max Shron provides simple guidelines for using data:

- What are you trying to achieve (context)?
- What will having the information accomplish that was impossible before (need)?
- What will it look like when you reach the outcome (vision)?
- By whom and how will the result be used and integrated into the company (outcome)?

A data and insights strategy is more about what you want to achieve and how you will use the data than the technical process of extracting it. When it comes to using data to provide a better brand experience for your audiences, it boils down to how well you know them and how you package information together. Whenever your brand touches them, it should feel so perfect for them that they couldn't imagine being with anyone else.

The stronger your customer profiles are, the more targeted your proposition will be to meet their needs. This means collecting information from the voice of the customer programmes. Cover all touch points, journeys, and channels that your customers go through, and include data from third-party review sites like TripAdvisor or Trustpilot. Also, consult non-competing brands that share your ideal personas to understand customer needs better.

Let's start approaching data management to add value to the brand by looking at data modelling techniques.

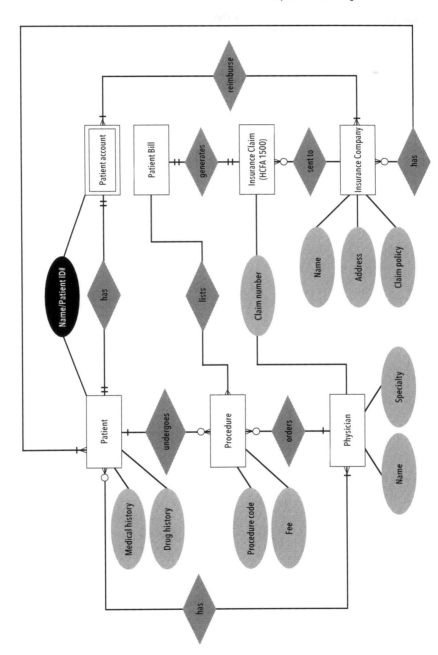

Data modelling

'The underlying benefit of creating a data model is that the data actually becomes understandable, others can read it and learn about it.'

Steve Hoberman

The biggest challenge a business can face when creating its data model is capturing the model's requirements correctly. Too often these requirements are vague or unknown, so spend time on agreeing the right requirements for your business.

Ask 'Do we really need to measure this, and why?' during the development process.

When you're building up the metrics that will form your data model, it is important to create a data dictionary to assign a single name and definition to each of the metrics. Get the business users and stakeholders to agree on the definitions and naming convention of each metric so that the dictionary can be signed off and documented as part of the data model. Where possible, have a central repository where the raw data is held, then use a single reporting application to produce reports.

Use your data dictionary, systems maps, and entity relationship diagrams to show the links between all the different systems and data sources, explaining what the equivalent value is in each system. The definitions are so different across different vendors and with so many different sources of data and different outputs, this will be an invaluable exercise to complete.

There are many different types of data that will contribute to the success of the business, but when it comes to the KPI scorecard, always measure what matters. Start from the brand promise, then you will ensure that you have a consistency that can be traced back to the overall company goals. Make sure the metrics for individual performances are correctly aligned and structured, so that people can be accountable for achieving the goals. It is important to have a blend of hard and soft measures, for example, the behaviours expected to meet the brand promise as well as the skills required in the team performance. When modelling data, you need to measure all the points throughout your audiences' journeys, not just the touch points.

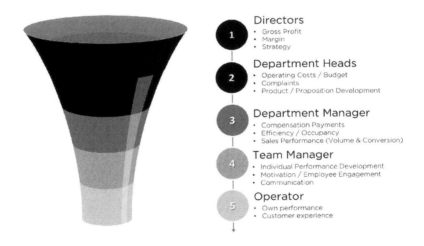

Data will generally fall into structured or unstructured categories. Structured data works well where the specific questions you ask are about intrinsic parts of the journey, because then you will be getting a natural response, giving you the ability to analyse answers to generic questions or outcomes. However, it is in the detail of unstructured data that the real gems are found.

We cannot keep surveying customers as a way of deciding whether they are happy with our products or services. Consumers are already suffering from survey fatigue. They now only tend to respond to survey requests if they are either really happy or really annoyed – at the extreme ends of the spectrum. On average, survey completion rates constitute 1–2% of all interactions,[73] so traditional metrics like NPS (net promoter score), CSAT (customer satisfaction score) and CES (customer effort score) are no longer reliable in understanding how good your customer experience is. We have to find a different way to gain an understanding of their satisfaction levels. Understand your customers' emotional engagement with your brand by listening. Technology allows you to monitor interactions to get an idea of when a customer touches your brand, and there is no limit to how many interactions you can review.

Record your customer calls and then use speech analytics tools to convert them to text, before pushing them through sentiment engines to listen to how emotionally engaged a customer is with your brand. Sentiment engines will tell you how a customer feels when they interact with you, which will give you much more information than the 1–2% survey response rate of customers, which does not constitute an accurate reflection of the overall experience you offer. If you bolt on your social media and digital conversations,

73 https://www.customerthermometer.com/customer-surveys/20-customer-survey-response-rate-facts-infographic/

you could be measuring 80% of your customer interactions, increasing the accuracy with which you identify how emotionally connected your brand customers are. A customer emotion score calculated from the emotional reactions to your brand captured through this 'always listening' approach is a much better reflection of your customer engagement, and reduces customer frustration with surveys. Data can give you lots of valuable nuggets about your customers if it is used in the right way. It's what you do with it that counts.

Creating the lightbulb moment

'If we have data, let's look at data. If all we have are opinions, let's go with mine.'

Jim Barksdale, former Netscape CEO

Data is only useful if it produces insight that enables you to create a better outcome for the customer, the employee, and the brand. Turning data into insights is about learning from the past, experimenting in the present, and predicting the future.

Let's take a look at each of those areas.

The past. When you were a child, did your parents ever say to you, 'I don't mind you making mistakes, so long as you learn from them'? The same learning approach applies to business. It's important to contextualise the data you have gathered when you're looking for reasons for success or failure in your business. Compare elements that affect the outcomes, such as time, market factors, and other metrics specific to your industry or success criteria. Dig deep to find the root cause of any problems by using a technique like the '5 Whys'[74]. Don't end up with valuable information locked up in dark data that is going ignored in the background.

Consulting and market research company Gartner Inc. describes dark data as 'information assets that organizations collect, process and store in the course of their regular business activity, but generally fail to use for other purposes.' The main way to avoid this is to make it easy to see important

---

74 https://en.wikipedia.org/wiki/5_Whys

information. Business leaders want insights to be set up so that they can quickly and easily see what the data is unveiling. The data guys will look at things in a much more technical way, so make sure your data modelling team is engaged in understanding how the brand promise feeds into scorecard requirements so they can format reports that create effective insights.

The present. When it comes to real time information, the speed at which insights arrive now makes them available at key decision points, enabling you to create powerful personalised customer propositions. This is especially the case when combined with existing data you already have about the customer. From mobile numbers to IP addresses, there are plenty of individual indicators you can store against a customer profile and use to create personalised experiences for them. Using the sentiment scores from previous interactions, you can see whom they like interacting with, or deliver offers related to their previous shopping habits. For example, a customer may like an espresso first thing in the morning, but prefer a latte at lunchtime, and with the addition of GPS, a coffee shop owner can send them location-related offers at times that match what they are likely to be considering.

This same kind of approach is often used with email marketing and proactive advertising where a relevant online search has been performed. Used effectively, customer segmentation can optimise the customer spend per transaction. Basing it on behaviours, purchasing habits, and 'other people like me' analytics, you have the capacity to sell much more than the customer originally intended to buy. Amazon's recommendation engine contributes 35% of all its revenue[26] and delivers sales conversions of up to 60%.[75] This approach can add significant benefit to your sales results.

Experiment with split-testing your approach to find out what data works best for your various personas. Some may prefer certain offers, formats, or content, while others may prefer video or a phone call. Use digital capabilities alongside traditional preferences in an effective CRM sequence to deliver relevant customer contact.

The future. Predicting the future sounds like a bit of a stretch, but you can use historical information, trend data, and mirroring to predict what may happen. This can be extremely powerful, but it can also be very dangerous and brand damaging if you get it wrong.

For example, a high-school girl was sent coupons through the post for maternity clothing and babywear. Furious, her father went to the store and shouted at the manager, 'Are you trying to encourage her to get pregnant?' This event happened when a statistician identified a 'pregnancy prediction' score from about twenty-five products which he could assign to each shopper. When he analysed the score, he could estimate the baby's due date and send coupons timed to specific stages of the pregnancy cycle. It turned out this young girl was actually in the early stages of pregnancy and hadn't yet broken the news to her father.[76]

75 http://fortune.com/2012/07/30/amazons-recommendation-secret/
76 https://www.forbes.com/sites/kashmirhill/2012/02/16/how-target-figured-out-a-teen-girl-was-pregnant-before-her-father-did/-4d6a62996668

You too can predict future behaviours and buying trends. Analytics allows businesses to be much smarter with their marketing, forecasting, and stock management throughout all phases of the supply chain, resulting in leaner operating costs and improved cash flow. Combining this with resource management and dynamic pricing can deliver healthy financial performance gains as well as giving a better customer experience.

Predicting the future can help businesses prevent disasters before they happen. Manufacturers can now see in data the stresses and strains on their products. This allows them to get in touch with the customers to perform preventative maintenance and ensure the product remains in good working order, reducing the hassle to the customer and elevating a brand's position. If that is a boiler in the coldest part of winter, then you have just saved a painful scenario from taking place.

Looking for trends in the data can uncover cost savings, areas that products can be improved upon, and scenarios that can be avoided with proactive action. It is important to identify where you are succeeding as well as failing, and to continue doing the right things while you test ideas in a safe zone. Once you have your insights, you then need to convert them into value in order for your business to experience the commercial benefits they bring.

Converting to value

'Vision without execution is hallucination.'

Thomas A. Edison

Once you have created insights from your data, you could end up with lots of potential areas to work on. How do you take them forward into continuous improvement initiatives and introduce them to the business?

If you can show senior stakeholders that the initiatives you have developed from your insights will fix some of their problems and enable some of their goals to become a reality, then you will find it easier to move these initiatives forward as a priority. There are three phases which will help you focus on this:

Phase 1: Fix the leaks and understand the opportunity. Lots of business problems could be avoided with a bit more care, employee empowerment, or a tweak to the current operating process. These problems will show up in your customer complaints and within any compensation that you give out. But these insights can be a fantastic way to turn the negatives into positives by fixing them first to reduce the pain being experienced by the brand. Data is your friend. By using analytics alongside some sensible performance management, you can allow your employees to be in charge of 'recovery control'. After a bad experience, 92% of customers would never consider going back to a business if their complaint was handled badly.[77] Fixing any

---

77 https://www.marketingweek.com/2016/02/15/how-dealing-with-a-complaint-properly-can-drive-brand-loyalty/

problems in this area can have a fantastic impact on customer retention and re-engagement of previous customers.

Phase 2: Be specific about whom to focus on. It is five to ten times cheaper to keep an existing customer than it is to attract a new one. By developing an understanding of a customer's retention propensity and margin analysis, you can see those who need to be managed in specific customer journeys and protect the long-term relationship with them. Get specific about the costs and profit for different types of customers to understand which personas you want to keep, which are the most valuable to you, and focus on making them happy. Use predictive personalisation from your analysis about their future behaviour and trends to deliver value beyond what they would expect.

Phase 3: Create scenarios to see what delivers the best long-term business results. Use your insights to look at different scenarios you want to explore, and identify where to invest time and effort for maximum gain. This could mean looking at new markets, new customer personas, or considering the items in your product range.

Do you know what the future value of your current customer base is? While your customers will differ in their buying cycles and priorities, your insights should still allow you to consider the customer lifetime value (CLV) of each group. I suggest using a four-box model like the one shown on the following page, which gives you a matrix showing where each customer sits in terms of value focus. You can then apply different approaches to their CRM depending on their personas.

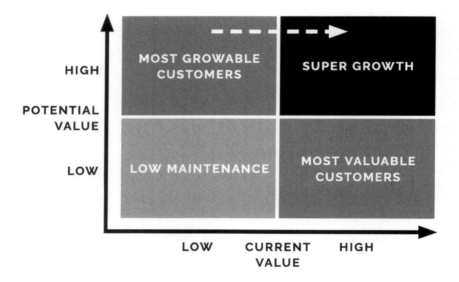

Don't let analysis cause paralysis: start taking action with the lowest-hanging fruit you find. Fix first and then get deeper into your customer groups before looking at the CLV for long-term results. What about the cost of doing all this? What about the cost of not doing it? Let's look at the areas to consider when assessing the return you will get on your investment.

What's it worth?

'The value of an idea lies in the using of it.'

Thomas A. Edison

Insights only have value when you take action on them. This requires the business to have a process to convert insights into initiatives and then change the business approach, but what about the cost of doing all this work? It is going to require some investment to make this a reality. But the cost of putting the brand experience forward as a priority will deliver much more than the investment you make.

Despite it being in the top three priorities of most CEOs today, there's still a lack of investment in dedicated customer experience (CX) programmes and budgets. In fact, 37% of businesses[78] are only just getting started with a formal CX programme, and even fewer are at an advanced stage of progress. Why is it, then, that something widely accepted as crucial to business success can be missed so frequently when it comes to investment? From my experience of talking to business leaders, there are many reasons, from a lack of understanding as to what is needed, to alternative business priorities getting the focus and funding that the business has to spend. Beyond Brand has pulled together a series of facts on the key areas of focus to help more companies take this crucial step. You can download it here: www.beyondbrand.co/the-roi-of-customer-experience/

---

[78] http://www.oracle.com/us/global-cx-study-2240276.pdf

ROI is key when you're gaining buy-in from stakeholders within your organisation and a common barrier to ensuring you get the required level of support and backing when your proposition is competing with other business priorities. The good news is that by improving the brand experience, you will generally help these other priorities and improve most key business metrics. But it is also important to instil belief. People in the business need to believe that changing the experience will achieve the impact you project, so give them a few quick wins at the beginning to get your promoters onside.

There are other areas where delivering a better brand experience will improve indirect cost factors. The cost of new product development, for instance, will reduce considerably once you are clear about who your ideal customers are and what they value. You will know what to develop from the insights that you have gleaned along the way. Equally, when new product-scoping exercises include what it will feel like to serve the customer, you will be considering the cost to serve within the margin model of each business case, which could affect profit forecasting. You can't just bolt the service element of a product on and expect it to feel market-leading. It needs to be part of the proposition development. In the same way, when you're building and selling a product, you need to consider the true cost of providing the brand experience to make sure the cost of sale includes this approach.

There are other indirect benefits, though, to investing in the brand experience as customer loyalty increases. Providing you have positioned your brand promise in the right way, customers will not only be happy to use you for their original purchases, but will also consider you for other products and services they need in their life. Once your brand is trusted, you are in their circle of trust. As long as the connection is relevant to the message of the brand, then increasing your share of wallet is a feasible option with these customers, and one that will boost the profitability of your relationship significantly. The cost in finding new customers is significant, so being able to sell additional products to existing customers will increase your margin substantially. Just remember that while your products and services don't need to be related to each other, they do all need to relate to your brand promise and higher purpose in order for your audiences to see the brand connection.

One other significant advantage to offering a brand experience is that your customers will become the biggest promoters of the brand. Think of them as an extension of your marketing toolkit. They will share how satisfied they are with the experience you provide, and if they are happy, their recommendations will supply you with lots of new customers. This plays an important part in growing a brand successfully.

Creating and protecting the brand experience constitutes one of the most crucial tasks for a company. Stories sell the brand experience, and the quality and consistency of those stories will be among the most valuable things you can invest in. When you factor in the savings to your operating costs, the ongoing benefit of retention loyalty, and the cost-efficient recommendations from happy customers, you can easily demonstrate to your stakeholders that the brand experience is much more valuable than marketing or advertising. Understanding data and insights to a point where you can introduce valuable actions will ensure the brand consistently delivers the constantly evolving demands of your audiences.

Take a break to complete Exercise 10 below before we move on to the next section to look at completing the 360° feedback loop and at the emotional triggers that affect our decision making.

EXERCISE 10

Take a look at your current metrics:

⚙ What do they tell you?

⚙ Who uses them?

⚙ How do they link to your brand promise and purpose?

⚙ Why do you want to know these metrics?

⚙ What action will you take from them?

⚙ Do they make the boat go faster?

⚙ Do they measure emotion or just performance?

What measures will you stop, start and continue using moving forward?

⚙ Create a balanced scorecard that covers all the measures you need to take to deliver your brand promise

⚙ How many of your products do your customers buy elsewhere?

⚙ What is the future value of your current customer base?

Avoid measuring everything:

⚙ Does the data move you closer to your vision?

⚙ Is personalisation a key part of your insight actions?

Reality check

'I think it's very important to have a feedback loop, where you're constantly thinking about what you've done and how you could be doing it better.'

Elon Musk

Do your customers think the experience you give is as good as you think it is? The various people, channels, and touch points in your business all have the potential to fall short of expectations. The gap between what a brand thinks is important versus what a customer and/or employee thinks is often large.

In 2005, Bain did a survey to see the discrepancy between what executives believed their customers thought about their experience and what their customers actually thought. Of the CEOs interviewed, 80% believed they delivered a superior customer experience, but only 8% of customers agreed.[79]

In 2015, the Customer Experience Benchmark Report by Execs In The Know made the same comparison again. This time, 79% of CEOs felt they were generally meeting their customers' needs, so roughly the same as ten years previously.[80] The customers' response had improved to 33%, which still left two thirds of customers believing that their needs were not being met. What could be more important than fixing that gap?

---

79 http://www.bain.com/bainweb/pdfs/cms/hotTopics/closingdeliverygap.pdf
80 http://www.execsintheknow.com/execs-in-the-know-copc-inc-release-2015-consumer-edition-in-customer-experience-management-benchmark-series/

Gaining a grasp on reality within your business is critical if you are to move the brand experience forward. Getting your senior team walking in the shoes of a customer or employee is an extremely powerful way to get change agreed and prioritised – much more powerful than just explaining in a presentation, or a proposal for improvements. It also does wonders in terms of respect and engagement if employees see that senior leaders care what they and their customers have to go through when interacting with the brand.

Views and trends shine through in the stories being told by your audiences, so take the time to listen to them. A relationship business must prioritise two-way communications and involve audiences in a consistent feedback loop to measure the progress of the improvements it is making. When both customers and employees have access to managers and directors, relationships blossom and trust in the brand builds.

Sharing data enables you to have transparent access to the real areas of importance and get a balanced view of strengths and weaknesses. Listen to the views of your customers and employees through various channels, measuring not just what people think about your brand, but also how it makes them feel. When you analyse these trends and use the two-way relationship, you can discuss what is important, demonstrating the progression you are making on the areas of priority. Empower people to get involved in the discussion, show that you are listening, and do something with the feedback. This all contributes to closing the feedback loop.

Complete the loop

'We all need people who will give us feedback. That's how we improve.'

Bill Gates

Listening is not the same as hearing. Listening requires concentration so that your brain processes the meaning of the words with the intention of understanding the other person and then reacting accordingly. When you merely hear someone without listening, it can lead to misunderstandings, missed opportunities, and a breakdown in the relationship.

Equally, how you react to feedback is crucial. Is all the feedback you gain through listening visible to all parties and shared among the team to improve how you deliver the brand experience? Do you operate with transparency, telling customers and employees what you will do with their feedback in a timely manner, even if you are not going to change anything? If someone has taken the time to give you the feedback then the least you can do is to respond and tell them the course of action and why. In order to keep the relationship positive, your business needs to take ownership of the feedback it gains and complete the 360° feedback loop.

It is essential to capture and organise information in a way that enables people to access it to improve their respective areas, and this is sometimes how valuable insights are found. You need an effective way of sharing the insights with the business so that the various teams can use the information to improve their respective areas. Sharing the impact of enhancements is a great way for engagement to rise, as well as your profits. If you can demonstrate the difference feedback has made to customer satisfaction results, then you are on your way to embedding a culture that values listening – what a great way of finding out what your people think of you and how you compare with your competitors. Keeping the relationship alive and conversation open enables you to use the feedback in your developments, predicting the future needs and desires of your audiences, while building brand engagement. Stay close to the most important people in your business: your audience.

Leveraging technology to work to your advantage will help you keep things simple. Ensure that once you have set up your operating model for managing feedback, it keeps delivering. Whether you are looking to gain 360° feedback from your employees or finding a way to understand the sentiment of your customers, there is a solution out there that can do it.

Below are a few suggestions to check out, but there are other options available. Make sure that whatever you choose works for your business and integrates with your existing technology infrastructure.

Employee

* https://www.etsplc.com/360-degree-feedback/
* https://www.decision-wise.com/360-degree-feedback/

Customer

* https://www.iperceptions.com
* http://www.rantandrave.com
* http://www.clarabridge.com
* https://www.salesforce.com/uk/products/einstein/overview/

Brand experience

Beyond Brand has its own solution for understanding how your brand experience scores today. We launched The Experience Map in 2016 (http://www.theexperiencemap.com) to measure the strength of your brand experience maturity across the same seven principles of the Beyond Brand methodology that we go through in this book. As a thank you for buying my book, I'm inviting you to visit http://www.beyondbrand.org/bb-book-free-experience-map/ and register your name and email, and I will send you a free access code worth £197.

Behavioural economics

'People exercise an unconscious selection in being influenced.'

T. S. Eliot

What does behavioural economics have to do with the brand experience? This is a huge subject area, so we will only scratch the surface of how behavioural economics can shape people's opinions of your brand, but if it is used correctly it can deliver amazing results.

Behavioural economics is based on identified theories about how humans make decisions, highlighting that people's perceptions of value and preferences are often not as rational as they may think. Most choices are not the result of careful consideration. Instead, people are influenced by what information is available to them and how it is presented, which can affect their instinctive reactions.

In our busy lives, we sometimes suffer from a distorted memory, which is affected by our physiological and emotional states. According to various sources, we make approximately 35,000 decisions a day, with only 5% being things we consciously think through.[81] The rest are automatic decisions based upon several known factors that psychologists have been studying since the early 1970s.

These can be broken down into six key theories.

---

81 https://www.neurosciencemarketing.com/blog/articles/subconscious-decision.htm

Rational choice. This behaviour assumes that we make choices based on weighing up the pros and cons of a situation – the costs versus the benefits, in the case of a purchase decision.

Prospect theory. This is our willingness to take risks when we're influenced by the way in which choices are framed, largely proving that we don't always make a rational choice.

Bounded rationality. This claims that the rationality of a decision depends on the environment we are in and the limits of the information available to us when we make the decision.

Dual system theory. This shows we have two ways of thinking, based on how and if we approach a situation – an automatic reaction (system 1 thinking) and a reflective reaction (system 2 thinking).

Temporal dimensions. The time we have available to make a decision affects the final decision we make, and it is an important dimension of our evaluations and preferences to consider.

Social dimensions. Humans do not always make decisions by themselves. We can be influenced by others when making our choices.

If you want to understand these six theories in greater detail, I recommend you check out Alain Samson's excellent article, 'An Introduction to Behavioral Economics'.[82]

---

82 https://www.behavioraleconomics.com/introduction-behavioral-economics/

Another interesting theorist is Robert Cialdini, whose fantastic book *Influence*, published in 1984, talks about how social forces affect our mindset. Cialdini describes six principles that have stood the test of time, which you should master if you want to look at influencing people's thoughts towards your brand.:

Reciprocity. When someone does us a favour, we usually feel obliged to repay them. Consultants often give away free advice to clients and prospects in the hope of paid business in the future, a principle often used by charities when seeking donations.

Consistency and commitment. The need for personal alignment. Making a commitment, especially if we do it publicly, makes a statement about what we will do or how we will behave on a consistent basis.

Social proof. People tend to look for acceptance or approval of our decisions by considering what others are doing, eg, the latest fashion or the etiquette of a golf club.

Liking. We generally like being around people whom we see as similar to ourselves, who share our interests, opinions, and personalities. We also love to receive praise and tend to like those who give it.

Authority. We tend to obey those in charge and trust respected authorities. If an expert gives a favourable opinion of a product or service, we are likely to accept their opinion.

Scarcity. We sometimes want what we can't have. The less available something is, the more people tend to want it.

By knowing various proven techniques and behavioural influences, we can introduce them into the way we market and present our brand, which can play a key part in whether someone chooses our brand or an alternative.

Cialdini explains that people often spend money on a product not because they need it, but because advertising stimulates them to feel as if they must have it while it is still available, otherwise they would kick themselves if they missed the opportunity. This is why car brands sell out limited-edition models for way above the list price, as people want to be seen as the first to have the latest model car from that brand.

A lot to consider?

If all that feels a little bit much to take in then don't worry too much about it. What it all boils down to is that the emotions and behaviours we experience can influence whether we choose to use a brand or not. They are definitely part of what makes customers and employees fall in love with brands. There are lots of other behavioural theories to consider in your design. The use of 'nudge' theory, for instance, can be very effective, and you may want to it explore further. Use your imagination and you will find ways to apply these techniques to your business model.

Before we end this chapter, I want to share an example from Cialdini's book of behavioural economics being used to make a commercial difference. It revolves around waiters looking at how they could increase their tips.

Minted

Of all the things that waiters could do to increase their tips, how high would you place giving mints on the list? In a study published in the *Journal of Applied Social Psychology*,[83] researchers compared a group of waiters giving mints with the bill to a group who were not giving any mints at all. Of the first group, some waiters gave the mints with the bill, making no mention of the mints. This increased tips by around 3% against the group giving no mints. However, when the waiters brought out two mints by hand and asked, 'Would anyone like some mints before they leave?' tips increased by 14%.

A final group brought out the bill along with a few mints, then after a short period came back with more mints, letting customers know that they had brought them in case anyone wanted more. In this test, the waiters saw a huge 21% increase in tips. Who would have thought that the way in which waiters offered mints to guests could increase the size of their tips by more than 20%?

Understanding behavioural economics gives you the ability to shape your brand experience, building your persona profiles by considering how your audiences react to these principles. This helps you to plan your customer and employee journey in a much more detailed way, considering how you make someone feel and how they are inclined to react to those emotions. This will play a major part in creating a brand that people fall in love with,

83   D. B. Strometz, B. Rind, R. Fisher, M. Lynn (2002), 'Sweetening the Till: The Use of Candy to Increase Restaurant Tipping', *Journal of Applied Social Psychology, 32* (2), 300–309.

helping to make your brand a commercial success. No pressure, then!

Before we move on to the final principle in the Beyond Brand methodology, please take some time to go through Exercise 11.

EXERCISE 11

Listening 360°

* When does your senior team have access to customer and employee discussions? How often?

* When do you have sessions where senior stakeholders walk in the shoes of a customer?

* What is the customer reality of your brand experience vs the expectation you have for the brand?

* How much of your feedback is captured centrally and shared in a transparent way?

* How often do you collect staff feedback to use on improving the employee experience?

Behavioural economics

* What examples of behavioural economics could you introduce into your customer journeys today?

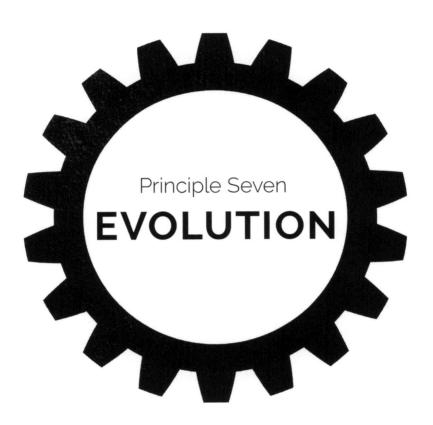

Principle Seven

EVOLUTION

Back to the future

'It is not the strongest of the species that survives, or the most intelligent; it is the one most capable of change.'

Charles Darwin

To sustain long-term success as a brand, you need to evolve constantly, so that you remain relevant to your audiences. With the exception of the first principle, purpose, the principles of the Beyond Brand methodology are all either evolving or in development. Your purpose, if it's strong and defined clearly in your brand promise, will never move. However, the other five principles need to be in a constant state of evolution if they are to develop alongside the expectations of your audiences. These could be subtle small changes that enhance a current offering, or they could be wholesale major changes, which totally transform the product range, like the introduction of iTunes and the iPod by a computer manufacturer.

In business, you are either moving forward or moving backwards; you cannot afford to stand still, otherwise someone else will take your place. Quite simply, businesses evolve or die. It doesn't matter how big or small a business is. Even the biggest brands that are relevant today are not immune from being replaced. Only 28% of the original FTSE 100 companies still exist today,[83] and 88% of the original Fortune

---

83 http://www.cityam.com/267704/ftse-100-history-index-has-changed-over-33-years

500 are gone.[84] The world evolves so quickly that you could be a leading brand in one decade and out of business in the next, if you do not invest in resources for future development and evolution. It doesn't even have to be that your product is no longer relevant either; some of the world's most valuable companies today don't even own anything. Airbnb is the world's largest provider of overnight accommodation, yet it doesn't own a single hotel.

History is littered with examples of lack of evolution resulting in a market leader being replaced by a newcomer. Let's take a look at a couple of examples from over the years that have gone down this path to emphasise the importance of evolution and the ability to be disrupted.

APPLE V NOKIA CASE STUDY

Back in the 1990s, if you had a mobile phone, it was probably a Nokia. According to Gartner, Nokia had a market share of 49.4% in 2007, before Steve Jobs launched the iPhone. Nokia, however, had become complacent with their software development and technology user experience. In the years that followed their market share dropped steadily, from 43.7% to around the 3% mark by the start of 2013. Nokia disappeared because of its failure to evolve its proposition. Meanwhile Apple, worth about $250bn in 2010, has gone from

---

84 http://www.aei.org/publication/fortune-500-firms-1955-v-2016-only-12-remain-thanks-to-the-creative-destruction-that-fuels-economic-prosperity/

strength to strength as it has constantly evolved its product range, and was worth over $908bn at the start of 2018.

BORDERS VERSUS AMAZON CASE STUDY

In the 1990s, Borders was a leading bookstore in the United States and around the world, with over 1,000 branches and a successful sales income of more than $1.5bn.[85] However, Borders made some bad strategic decisions, which led to its downfall in 2011.

Borders outsourced its online business to Amazon in 2001, and for the next seven years, Amazon took all its customers on to its own platform. Choosing to ignore the internet, Borders instead invested in store expansion at a time when the internet was starting to impact retail footfall. After failing to invest in e-readers and technology, Borders over-invested in the CD and DVD sections of its business, just as those products were declining due to iTunes downloads and subscription channels like Spotify.

Since Borders folded, Amazon has grown to a market valuation of over $700bn, and is still growing every month.[86]

---

85 http://www.fundinguniverse.com/company-histories/borders-group-inc-history/
86 https://ycharts.com/companies/AMZN/market_cap

Evolution is crucial to long-term success, no matter how big or small your business is. Ensure you have a long-term development strategy to stay ahead of the competition in decades from now. It also pays to understand market trends, future developments, and opportunities to buy the right companies at the right time as investments. Yahoo twice had a chance to buy Google, once in 1998 when the two founders wanted just $1m so they could continue their studies at Stanford, and then again in 2002, when they wanted $5bn for the company. Yet they walked away from both opportunities, only to see it flourish while Yahoo was finally sold to Verizon in 2016 for just $4.6bn. As if that wasn't bad enough, they also apparently had a chance to buy Facebook in 2006 for $1bn, but failed after lowering their valuation.

The growth of companies to that magical $1bn valuation that turns them into unicorns is happening more quickly than we have experienced in the past. Much of the time these are companies that don't even own any products. Welcome to the age of the experience brokers.

The experience brokers

'Every business today is a media and tech business, irrespective of what their primary business purpose is.'

Tom Foremski

Today's biggest companies don't own anything. All the recent additions are experience-driven businesses. The ultra-brands, which didn't exist twenty years ago – Facebook, Google, Uber, and Airbnb – are all brands that have enhanced the way we go about getting what we want. They are virtual brokers of services who have disrupted traditional industries, and have become the most valuable brands of today. Just look at how the swing of power has moved throughout the ten years since 2006 in terms of the most valuable brands. Back in 2006 you had traditional oil, engineering and banking brands that made up the top five. In 2016 that had moved to tech and media businesses that help provide us with experience solutions that make our lives easier!

It doesn't end with just the world's most valuable brands, either. The term 'unicorn' was coined in 2013 to mean a privately owned start-up valued at over $1 billion. Aileen Lee chose the mythical animal to represent the statistical rarity of such a venture because back in 2013 there were only thirty-nine companies that claimed the tag. As of March 2017, there were 223 unicorns, according to TechCrunch, and that list is growing fast. *Harvard Business Review* carried out a study looking into the rise of the unicorn company that determined that start-ups formed between 2012 and 2015 were growing in valuation twice as fast as companies formed between 2000 and 2013. Not content with just being unicorns, some of these ventures are now worth tens of billions and therefore claim the tag of 'decacorn'. Which company will become the first 'hectocorn' by being the first privately owned venture worth more than one hundred billion dollars?

A full list of unicorns can be found on Fortune's website http://fortune.com/unicorns/. Here are the current top five:

- Uber (car sharing/travel – $62.5bn), started in San Francisco, United States
- Alipay (payment platform – $60bn), started in China
- Xiaomi (smartphone/consumer electronics – $45bn), started in China
- Didi Chuxing (car sharing/travel – $33.7bn), started in China
- Airbnb (home sharing/travel – $31bn) started in San Francisco, United States

Three of these companies are part of the recent trend of the 'sharing economy'. This concept of sharing personal resources has been adopted through the economic downturn of recent years, making way for these start-ups to be created as millennial generations learned to be more economical with their spending habits.

Looking through the companies on the unicorn list, we can see that many are taking traditional industries or solutions and disrupting them into a new way of working, a new way of experiencing. This, coupled with the new digital economy, is driving a rate of change that we have never seen before.

What the companies will look like in five or ten years' time will be drastically different from how they look today. This will force existing businesses to either evolve or die, in the same way that companies who previously dominated the financial markets have now disappeared or evolved. To ignore this need for change will be fatal.

Your business will have to buy the competition out of the market if it has stolen a march on you from a development and innovation perspective, or be creative enough to ensure you stay ahead of the market in the first place. Both can be successful strategies, but the latter is the most cost effective. So, what does it take to have a creative DNA in your company culture?

Creative DNA

'Innovation is change that unlocks new value.'

Jamie Notter

If you are serious about having creative DNA as part of your brand, then innovation needs to be integral to its culture, people, and working practice. Dedicate time, resource, and budget to long-term evolution, research, development, and testing to build innovation and creativity into your culture. For example, Google allows 20% of its employees' time to be spent on projects and ideas they are passionate about, outside of their normal roles. Alternatively, you could introduce regular events to allow your teams to come up with inspirational ideas on how your brand can innovate and progress the industry you work within. Some companies have even gone as far as setting up dedicated departments to focus exclusively on innovation. If you tackle the biggest problems in your industry before others do, then you'll stay ahead.

However you do it, it is important that you invite everyone to be in the creative club. Some of the best ideas come from unexpected sources and the culture of inclusion is very powerful in engaging everyone, rather than just the few. Adopt a culture of 'just imagine if…' while embracing evolution within the boundaries of your brand promise. People tend to work best in this culture when they have a clear expectation of where the boundaries start and finish. My advice is to link any evolution time to your brand promise and purpose, but don't constrain people too much.

Allowing people permission to fail is a crucial part of embracing evolution. What would you do if you weren't afraid? If you want people to be creative and think outside the box then they have to feel protected when they're going into this headspace. Give them the freedom to test and learn, but ensure you put stages in place to ensure you achieve an ROI of your time, money, and resources. Give people the freedom to be at the centre of evolving things, while guiding them to move fast and break things in the early stages of the process. That way, people prioritise the right ideas without crushing their creativity. Prove concept on a small stage, and then pitch for further investment.

The senior management team needs to show a keen interest in the culture of evolution. However, it is important that they play the right role in progressing the ideas. The management structure involved in the innovation teams should be relatively flat, with employees empowered to make the progress required to get to each stage. There needs to be a clear understanding of how progression of ideas will happen in your organisation and the governance that is wrapped around it. This ensures people respect the stages and process to work through in order to get approval to carry on with development. Equally, they need to know when an idea is dead and not just dormant, perhaps by using a RAG (red, amber, green) status, a prioritisation scorecard, or a dedicated communication structure. Otherwise the people who are passionate about it still cling on to hope that it might get approved and therefore dedicate effort to it. If the process is transparent, your teams will buy into it more readily. Play the role of a senior approver in the progression of ideas, creating clear checkpoints where the ideas are discussed. Step in, give the verdict as to how or if the ideas will progress, then butt out.

Reacting to change

> *'Transformation means that you're really fundamentally changing the way the organization thinks, the way it responds, the way it leads.'*
>
> **Lou Gerstner**

When you want to transform your business or move direction, people will need to understand why things are changing. If the change is managed well, it should feel natural – evolution rather than revolution. Effective evolution should not feel radical at the time. Only when you look back should it feel like you have moved a long way and made many improvements.

 PORSCHE 911 CASE STUDY

Porsche first introduced the 911 in 1963, and although we have had seven different model shapes and over ten variants, it has stuck to its distinctive look and heritage.

What Porsche has done well over the years is to evolve its product, improving it regularly and ensuring it remains one of the best drivers' cars that money can buy. This has kept it relevant, desirable, and achieving the needs of the target audience better than any other manufacturer.

When you focus on evolution, it is critical that you keep the personas of your most valuable people and your brand promise at the forefront of any decisions. Even if you are going in a totally different direction in terms of products/ services, so long as those two things are key, you will remain relevant as a brand consideration for your target audiences.

Innovation is a very different matter to evolution, although there should still be a relevant connection your purpose and brand promise. Innovation is about entering new ground; doing things differently to how they have been done. This isn't diversification, either. I'm talking about innovating in a way that disrupts an industry or causes an audience to take a different approach to a solution – renting out bedrooms as an alternative to hotels, or using contactless payment methods rather than chip and pin to buy things. These are advances that have disrupted traditional ways of working, but are now second nature to the majority of us in our everyday lives. Advances in technology and analytics will no doubt continue to serve as enablers, allowing us to do things better, faster, and more cheaply than we have done in the past, but those who change the way we approach a sector or find solutions to the most hated problems will be the ones who make a step change in their industries.

Chris Maloney, a smart marketer from Australia, created Maloney's 16% rule,[87] arguing that you can influence the innovators (2.5%) and the early adopters (13.5%) with your

---

87   https://innovateordie.com.au/2011/11/01/the-16-rule-the-secret-to-accelerating-diffusion-of-innovation-presentation-slides/

proposition by using Cialdini's scarcity approach. Once you have got these audience personas on board, you switch your marketing and media approach from scarcity to social proof to bring on board the early and late majority adopters.

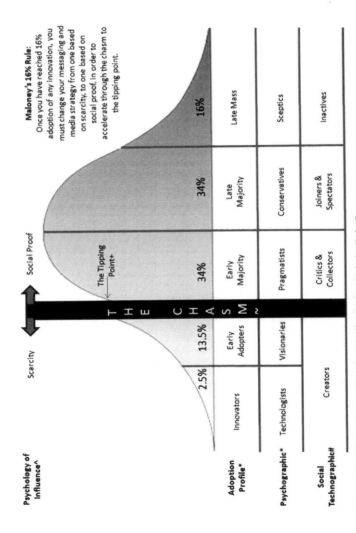

Accelerating Diffusion of Innovation: Maloney's 16% Rule©

Maloney's 16% Rule: Once you have reached 16% adoption of any innovation, you must change your messaging and media strategy from one based on scarcity, to one based on social proof, in order to accelerate through the chasm to the tipping point.

Psychology of Influence^ : Scarcity — Social Proof

THE CHASM≈ : The Tipping Point+

	2.5%	13.5%	34%	34%	16%
Adoption Profile*	Innovators	Early Adopters	Early Majority	Late Majority	Late Mass
Psychographic*	Technologists	Visionaries	Pragmatists	Conservatives	Sceptics
Social Technographic#	Creators		Critics & Collectors	Joiners & Spectators	Inactives

^ Robert Cialdini *Everett Rogers #Forresters ~Geoffrey Moore + Malcolm Gladwell

When you're introducing innovation and evolution, moving people through the change curve will be a vital part of your success. Only by transitioning from the old to the new carefully and in the right timeframe will you ensure that hearts and minds come on the journey as well as the changes to technology and processes. Communicating with your audiences is key in taking people through the transition, so do so on a continuous basis. If you rarely introduce change and communicate with the same frequency, then you will struggle to evolve without casualties. What can we expect from the next generation of change and where will evolution take us next?

The next generation

'The best way to predict your future is to create it.'

Abraham Lincoln

Who can predict the future? If we could do that, we would likely find ways to make money and create a successful brand. What will happen in the next five to ten years? Where should we be focusing our effort, and what is the next big thing coming our way that we need to be thinking about?

Some of the radical changes haven't been discussed yet, while others will only affect certain industries. Customers will start to benchmark brands by the ones that make their lives more enjoyable and give them better use of their time, so if someone hasn't disrupted your industry yet, start thinking how you could do it. Companies are going to have to stand out and think differently to all the rest if customers are going to be shocked into changing their default options.

APPLE CASE STUDY

Apple's 'Think Different' relaunch campaign highlighted that it wanted to succeed and stand out, not be one of the 'me too' brands. By doing so, it threw away conventional methods of doing things and introduced concepts that were very different to anything people had seen before. From transparent brightly coloured iMacs showing their insides to the creation of devices so simple a two-year-old can use them,

Apple has stretched the boundaries with amazing products, wonderful packaging, distinctive store experiences, and clever product launches that generate hype and excitement. It has made things easier to use, more intuitive to pick up and more of an experience. The company has also had the confidence to look beyond what everyone else is doing to create its own path. It has focused on what life could be like if it removed the constraints and frustrations that other devices are offering.

Apple has got it right, and in doing so, it has created the most valuable company on the planet.

The impact of next generation companies and entrepreneurs has changed the way we interact with brands and choose our favourites from the wide selection we have these days. The generations have changed their priorities as well now, moving from a desire to own big-ticket items to a rented model. Audiences now value experiences above living in debt to own traditional things such as a house or a flash car. When these things can be rented and owning them feels way out of reach, the choice of what a good brand experience looks like is very different.

Technology has already introduced smart devices and those devices are getting smarter and more integrated all the time. The future will be in a connected world, with IoT and machine learning growing into our lives alongside AI and virtual assistants. Virtual reality will become the norm, changing the way we buy products for ever. Try them out virtually before you buy them, to experience them before you decide.

Or don't buy them at all, just have the virtual equivalent. Not so much Total Recall, but a different experience for many industries. From entertainment to automotive, retail to holidays, could it even be the end of dating sites as we know it? We will enter into the realm of automation in our lives. Software will learn from human interaction, then automate and replace the need for human workers to do certain tasks. Human interaction will then be reserved for more complex queries and emotional connections.

Less opportunity for contact will mean less margin for error, so you need to make it count when you do interact. Make sure digital relationships trigger the same emotional reactions as traditional relationships as the balance tips further into the digital world. Fewer opportunities to build meaningful relationships will mean placing more importance on creating the right brand experience. Consumers will prefer auto corrective, preventative maintenance and autonomous appliances to automate anything that can give them the hours back from the technology advancements. One thing's for sure: the pressure to produce great products and services designed to make people's lives easier has never been as strong as it is about to become. Our roles will be to make the experiences as smart as the technology that is driving them. Technology should just be the enabler, one that allows you to create a better way of delivering your products or services. A way that allows evolution to take place to remove frustrations, free up more time and enhance lives by being authentically different. The authentic bit is very important. Stick to your purpose, stick to your brand promise, and evolve new ways of differentiation.

Evolution brings the Beyond Brand methodology to a close, but before we summarise how all the principles work seamlessly in a model which is timeless, please take a look at the exercise below to see how future-focused your business is.

EXERCISE 12

- ✿ DNA den – how can you create space for innovation in your business?

- ✿ Reaction time – how do you currently take people through the change curve?

- ✿ What's next? Think differently. Now is already taken care of, so what is the next game changer in your industry?

- ✿ What are the problems in your industry that no one can solve?

- ✿ What is the one thing you could introduce that would be so valuable that people would change their behaviour to buy it?

- ✿ How would you describe your culture today in its approach to innovation?

Conclusion: Putting It All Together

Connecting the cogs

We have covered a lot over the seven principles of the Beyond Brand methodology. Individually, these principles are important, but when you put them together, you get a complete review and design of the brand experience.

In the same way that Tesla brought together the established components of the motor car and the lithium-ion battery to create something more useful, the Beyond Brand methodology brings together the seven most important principles to deliver the right experience. And how they fit together in the model shows how interdependent they are with each other.

A solid **purpose** and brand promise are the foundations upon which everything else depends and will make you different from all the 'me too' brands. The next five principles connect solidly with your purpose. You will identify which **audiences** will be attracted to your brand once you have a clear definition of whom you are there to serve. The **approach** you take to reach your audiences will be crucial to ensure they know how good a fit you are for them and how easy you are to do business with. The **channels** you use will be designed with your customers in mind and seamlessly integrated so that the customer journeys are convenient and via the methods they want to use. Your **offers** will feel distinctly different and personalised to the audiences that you specialise in. Once you know these audiences better than anyone else, use the insights from their feedback to your **advantage** to create compelling propositions and shape your future developments.

Finally, consider your **evolution**. Constantly finding solutions to the problems that frustrate your audiences, all built around your purpose and brand promise, will ensure you remain the default choice and stand the test of time. All this will be built around the purpose and brand promise which will remain constant as your guiding principle.

These seven principles will guide you as you work through the three phases of discovery, design and delivery. They are timeless. The future channels may be different and your offer may change, but the principles will still remain the solid steps to creating a fantastic brand experience.

If you understand the seven principles, then you can apply them to your business through the teams you have today.

This opens up the ability for companies of all shapes and sizes to deliver a great brand experience. Previously only the corporate giants could justify spending six-figure sums on the experience. Now, even the smaller businesses can use this methodology to deliver competitive advantage and that has to be good for the economy. At Beyond Brand, we believe that everyone deserves to have a great experience. I hope you now take this forward into your business and deliver success to your audiences.

If you haven't done so already, I recommend you start with completing the experience map. This will give you a baseline as to where your brand experience is today against the seven principles, as well as guiding you on your initial areas of focus. Then you will be in a position to start redesigning your experience using the knowledge you've gleaned from this book.

If you would like to learn more about how Beyond Brand could help your business transform its brand experience by using this methodology, book a free thirty-minute call with my team today. Please visit https://calendly.com/craigbb/30min/ to find a slot in our diaries.

Here's to creating amazing experiences. Make sure you enjoy the journey.

Further Reading

Ted Matthews, *Brand: It ain't the logo. It's what people think of you*, CreateSpace Independent Publishing Platform (26 Jun. 2012)

Simon Sinek, *Start With Why*, Penguin; 01 edition (6 Oct. 2011)

Robert Cialdini, *Influence: The Psychology of Persuasion*, Harper Business; Revised ed. edition (1 Feb. 2007)

Matthew Dixon, *The Effortless Experience*, Portfolio Penguin (26 Sept. 2013)

Seth Godin, *Purple Cow: Transform Your Business by Being Remarkable*, Penguin (27 Jan. 2005)

Philip Hesketh, *How to Persuade and Influence People*, Capstone; Revised, Updated ed. edition (16 Sept. 2010)

Matthew Dixon, *The Challenger Customer*, Portfolio Penguin (3 Sept. 2015)

Shep Hyken, *The Amazement Revolution*, Greenleaf Book Group LLC (28 July 2011)

Max Shron, *Thinking with Data*, O'Reilly Media; 1 edition (3 Feb. 2014)

Andy Bounds, *The Jelly Effect*, Capstone; Revised, Reprint edition (10 Aug. 2010)

Matthew Dixon, *The Challenger Sale*, Portfolio Penguin (7 Feb. 2013)

Don Hales & Derek Williams, *Wow, That's What I Call Service*, Ecademy Press (2 July 2007)

Philip Hesketh, *Persuade*, Capstone; 1 edition (16 Oct. 2015)

Jay Baer, *Hug Your Haters*, Portfolio (1 Mar. 2016)

Jim Collins, *Good to Great*, Random House Business; 1st edition (4 Oct. 2001)

Jim Rohn, *The Art of Exceptional Living*, Nightingale Conant (1 Jan. 1994)

Dan Ariely, *Predictably Irrational*, Harper (1 Jun. 2009)

Richard H Thaler & Cass R Sunstein, *Nudge: Improving Decisions About Health, Wealth & Happiness*, Penguin (5 Mar. 2009)

J.T. O'Donnell, *Careerealism*, Dog Ear Publishing (30 April 2008)

Acknowledgements

This book is the result of some long days of writing, which couldn't have been achieved without the help and support of some wonderful people.

I would sincerely like to thank:

My two amazing children, Finlay and Isla, who are my world. I hope Daddy makes you proud and we continue to have lots of fun and laughter along the journey.

My wonderful wife, Lou. Thank you for ensuring the home remains a smooth-running machine and being an amazing mum to our children while I chase my dreams.

My parents Rita and David and my grandma Connie for always believing in me, even when I couldn't see it myself.

My second (much larger) family for continuing that support and interest as I went through the rollercoaster of writing the book – Wendy, Rob, Roger, Diane, Sam, Amy, Rachel, Ole and Steve.

Lucy, Joe and Siobhan, the amazing team at Rethink Press, for your help in making this book the best version it could possibly be.

I couldn't have got the book down on paper, nor kept going throughout all the challenges along the way, without the dedicated support of the wonderful Sarah Ward. Thank you for your patience and commitment in reading over and over the various versions of the book that were passed your way, as well as your belief in taking this concept into a whole new market.

Frea O'Brien, for your insistence that the book needed to be written in order for Beyond Brand to get the exposure that it deserved.

The team of people who get Beyond Brand looking and sounding as good as it does in all of our work – Kate Curry, Jess Barker, Alona Stukalova, Katarina Lukic, Ian Brodie, Dipesh Palmer, Zubair Russell, and Emma Nutbean.

Steven Oddy, Richard Burch, and Claire Meddings – the team at Sotech for helping me to create the Experience Maps.

Aston Business School, Coventry & Warwickshire Innovation Programme, Natwest Entrepreneurial Accelerator, and the Institute of Directors for the fantastic support, backing, and guidance you have given Beyond Brand.

Matt Crabtree, Ian Brodie, Matthew Kimberley, Mark Whitehand, and Elinor Perry-Hall – my business mentors who have taken me under their wings and helped me refine this raw potential into something valuable.

Words cannot express what an outstanding job Rachel Ollerenshaw and the team at Molly Olly's Wishes do to create amazing experiences for children who have been dealt bad cards. I hope Beyond Brand can help you to achieve your goals by doubling the number of children you help each year.

Chris and Nikki Foreman, Wayne Lidgbird, Richard Harley (Loaf), Carl Bannister, Jeff Chapman, Martin Verity, and Hazel de Kloe. You are the best friends anyone could need in life and I love you all dearly.

Finally, to the awesome clients and businesses I get to work with every single day. Thank you for choosing Beyond Brand and for having the faith and courage to invest in the experience of your brands.

The Author

Craig McVoy has over twenty years' experience of working with some of the most admired brands in the world, helping them to shape their customer experience strategy and operational excellence. Starting in customer-facing roles, progressing through middle management, and then serving as an executive director, Craig has faced the same challenges he helps businesses overcome today. Now an established speaker and author on the topic of customer experience, Craig has worked with the likes of John Lewis, BMW, Mercedes-Benz, Jaguar, Land Rover, Audi, LV=, RBS, and Direct Line.

The Beyond Brand Group was formed in June 2016, bringing together Consort, Beyond Brand and The Experience Maps, all of which had been launched by Craig. While writing the synopsis for this book, Craig realised that he used his own unique methodology to help create brand experience. By systemising the methodology, he was able to structure it into seven key principles that could be introduced to small and medium-sized businesses. Craig now runs the three businesses as the CEO.

Beyond Brand helps companies deliver commercial results by improving their customer and employee experience. Following the Beyond Brand methodology, business leaders can walk through seven simple principles to create a fantastic brand experience.

Consort is a specialist customer experience consultancy, which has been operational since October 2014, when Craig left an illustrious corporate career to set up his own business. Consort works with corporate halo clients, helping them design and develop their customer and employee experiences to increase brand value and profitable growth.

The Experience Maps were created in 2016 to add research and benchmarking to the toolkit used by both Consort and Beyond Brand. Using the Beyond Brand methodology, The Experience Maps measure the strength of your brand experience maturity across the seven principles through an online diagnostic portal. Available in three different versions, they produce a summary of where your brand experience is today through the lens of the leadership teams, the employees, and the customer.

Links:

⌂ http://www.beyondbrand.co

⚙ http://www.theexperiencemap.com

in https://uk.linkedin.com/in/craigmcvoy

🐦 https://twitter.com/CMcVoy

Printed in Great Britain
by Amazon